A theory for wealth of nations

Market economics overturns Adam Smith and Karl Marx

S. Kalyanaraman

Sarasvati Research Center

2012

Library of Congress Control Number 2012923311

ISBN-10: 0982897162
978-0-9828971-6-4

Printed in the USA.

First paperback printing: 2012

Table of Contents

Economic theories & Political economy 4

Market capitalization of listed companies (% of GDP) in world 31

Global crisis and the decline of market fundamentalist form of capitalism 35

Network of corporate control of economic activity in the globe 43

The network corporate 51

Less than 1% of Companies in Control 54

Global capitalism attempts to make society subservient 57

Economic history of two millennia 61

A relativist theory for wealth of nations 99

Śreṇi dharma: coping with greed and corruption 147

Upholding the earth for wealth 159

Five dimensional economic model of Subramanian Swamy 209

Social capital model of Vaidyanathan 214

Household economics 220

-- Rebuilding economic theory founded on the household

Market fundamentalism needs the corrective of a global ethic 227

European Community and Indian Ocean Community as Rāṣṭram, grouping of nations 241

Index 245

End Notes 247

Economic theories & Political economy

It is not about *laissez-faire* versus government intervention. Economic theories of capitalism or communism are irrelevant for today's political economy.

Laissez-faire capitalist has yielded to the market. While the term 'market' refers to many systems or institutions which engage in exchange, this work refers to stock markets which exchange shares in corporations, derivatives, bonds (debt instruments).

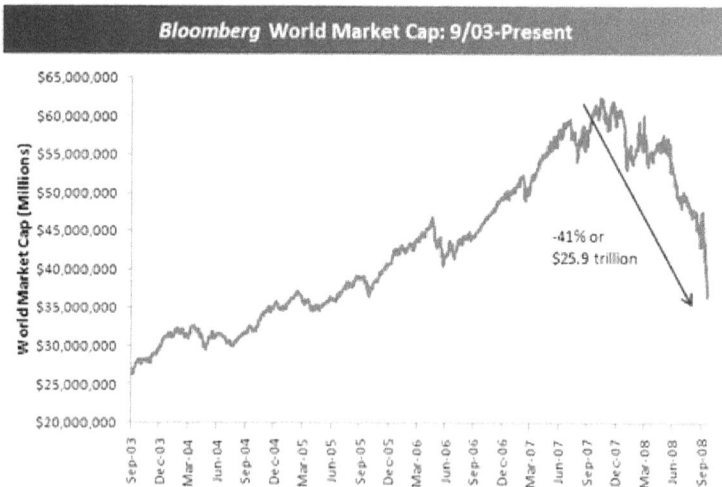

Bloomberg World Market Cap: 9/03-Present

-41% or $25.9 trillion

According to one estimate, $36.6 trillion was the size of the world stock market in October 2008 and derivatives market was estimated at about $791 trillion.[1]

World Wealth vs World Derivatives 1998-2007

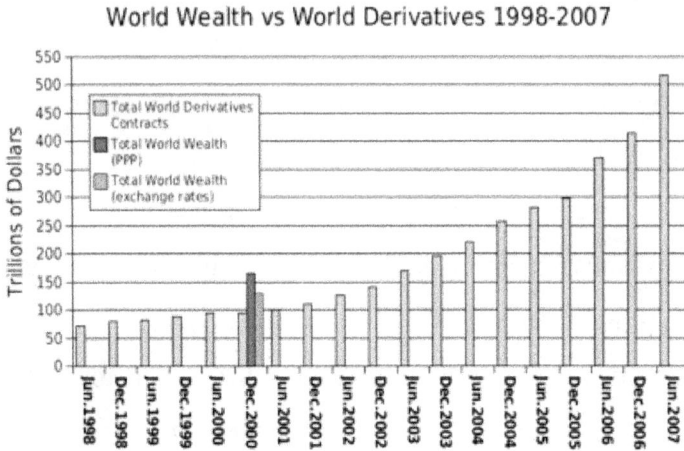

Total world derivatives from 1998–2007[2] compared to total world wealth in the year 2000

Systemic risk is on the rise, note Nicholas Chan et al.: "Systemic risk is commonly used to describe the possibility of a series of correlated defaults among financial institutions---typically banks---that occur over a short period of time, often caused by a single major event. However, since the collapse of Long Term Capital Management in 1998, it has become clear that hedge funds are also involved in systemic risk exposures. The hedge-fund industry has a symbiotic relationship with the banking sector, and many banks now operate proprietary trading units that are organized much like hedge funds. As a result, the risk exposures of the hedge-fund industry may have a material impact on the banking sector, resulting in new sources of systemic risks. In this paper, we attempt to quantify the potential impact of hedge funds on systemic risk by developing a number of new risk measures for hedge funds and applying them to individual and aggregate hedge-fund returns data. These measures include: illiquidity risk exposure, nonlinear factor models for hedge-fund and banking-sector indexes, logistic regression analysis of hedge-fund liquidation probabilities, and aggregate measures of volatility and distress based on regime-switching models. Our preliminary findings suggest that the hedge-fund industry may be heading into a challenging period of lower expected returns, and that systemic risk is currently on the rise."[3]

The real risk is that derivative as a risk insurance is itself the rism. "A hedged position can become unhedged at the worst times, inflicting substantial losses on those who mistakenly believe they are protected."[4]

Buyers and sellers are largely institutions (e.g., pension funds, insurance companies, mutual funds, index funds, exchange-traded funds, hedge funds, investor groups, banks and various other financial institutions).[5] The derivatives market cap is 10 times the GDP of the globe and equals $100,000 for each of the 7 billion inhabitants of the planet. "According to the most recent report[6] from the U.S. government's Office of the Comptroller of the Currency (OCC), the total value of derivatives has increased approximately 1000% since 1996, and 250% since 2006 (see graph on page 12 of the OCC report). Derivatives continued their rapid climb even in the midst of the global recession that started in 2008. Most disturbing is the fact that 95% of all U.S. derivatives are monopolized by just five megabanks and their holding companies... Thankfully, politicians are slowly becoming aware of the huge risk of the derivatives bubble and are taking steps in the right direction[7], but there is a long way still to go. And the financial speculation tax has yet to gain traction."[8]

"Some of the most basic forms of Derivatives are Futures, Forwards and Options. Futures and Forwards. As the name suggests, futures are derivative contracts that give the holder the opportunity to buy or sell the underlying at a pre-specified price some time in the future. They come in standardized form with fixed expiry time, contract size and price. Forwards are similar contracts but customisable in terms of contract size, expiry date and price, as per the needs of the user. Options. Option contracts give the holder the option to buy or sell the underlying at a pre-specified price some time in the future. An option to buy the underlying is known as a Call Option. On the other hand, an option to sell the underlying at a specified price in the future is known as Put Option. In the case of an option contract, the buyer of the contract is not obligated to exercise the option contract. Options can be traded on the stock exchange or on the OTC market."[9]

Dictatorship of the proletariat has yielded to the market. Speculative, risk-taking market is the mantra, rendering economics of Adam Smith and Karl Marx not as rival but irrelevant antideluvian theories.

Economic science is not dismal, the market behavior driven by speculation and betting makes today's Market Economics is dismal.

Market economics is the new *laissez-faire* specter haunting the globe. The dismal economic thought, structure and theory means that both *Adam Smith's Wealth of Nations* and Karl Marx's *Communist Manifesto* are overturned.

A possible solution to the specter of market fundamentalism lies in an ancient theory still practiced in many parts of the globe, the theory of wealth of nations created by social capital.

In the 19th century, Victorian historian Thomas Carlyle devised the derogatory alternative name for economics and called it 'dismal science'. Though the term was in the context of Thomas Malthus' dismal prediction of mas starvation caused by mismatch between population growth and food production growth, Carlyle argued[10] that reintroducing slavery would be morally superior to relying on the market forces of supply and demand.

This is not about debunking economics.[11] This is about the disappointing failures of Adam Smith and Karl Marx as forecasters of economic historical imperative for sustaining the wealth of nations for the benefit of the present and future generations. This sustenance of wealth is referred to as *abhyudayam* – as one of the objectives of *dharma-dhamma* -- in Hindu thought.

9

Adam Smith[12] and Karl Marx[13] are failures as thinkers and will turn in their graves if they encounter today's political economy. They will find that 'laissez-faire' economics or 'capitalism' has yielded place to 'market economics' and that 'market economics' has gobbled up virtually all remnants of 'dictatorship of the proletariat', creating instead 'dictatorship of the market'[14]. The dismal failure of the proletariat is exemplified by the collapse of the Berlin wall, dismemberment of the Soviet Union and emergence of Chinese capitalism (even if it is characterized as 'pre-capitalist agrarian system' in the jargon of the communist manifesto which lies in tatters – both as a theoretical alternative economic theory and as a transient practical demonstration of the demise of capitalism).

In today's political economy, the individual is no longer the 'sovereign' maker of economic decisions. The omnipresent 'market' determines economic decisions in collaboration with the state, using the state as a coercive axis economic power. The state has not withered away despite Marxist prognosis of the inexorable march of capitalism-communism and there is no trace of any dialectical synthesis. The state has been gobbled up and enslaved by 'market economics'. The dismal state of affairs is exemplified by a President of the United States of America acting as an agent of 'market economics' and not acting at the service of free peoples of America who made him President.

A Cluetrain manifesto[15] written in 1999 by Rick Levine et al stated: "A powerful global conversation has begun. Through the Internet, people are discovering and inventing new ways to share relevant knowledge with blinding speed. As a direct result, markets are getting smarter—and getting smarter faster than most companies." The conversation went nowhere and didn't even cause a ripple in the market, where it is speculation and hedging together with credit swapping and invention of new financial derivatives as usual to reinforce the dictatorship of the market.

"The most common types of derivatives are futures; forwards, which are futures traded outside of a regular exchange; options, which are the right to buy or sell something at a specified date and price; and swaps, contracts involving an exchange of assets or payments. In recent years, a bewildering variety of derivatives have been developed. One kind that played a central role in the financial crisis are credit default swaps, which are in essence a form of insurance policy, and whose value swings with the fiscal health of the transaction or asset it is written to cover. Swaps and other derivatives were often sold and resold in ways that attenuated the link between a party who created the thing of value being covered, and helped disguise the level of debt financial institutions were taking on. In the later stages of the housing boom, credit default swaps written in reference to mortgage-backed bonds were themselves bundled into financial instruments, known as synthetic CDOs, or collateralized debt obligations. Investors buying CDOs were essentially placing a wager on whether bonds held by someone else would turn a profit or fail. At the end of 2008, the Bank for International Settlements in Switzerland estimated the face value of all derivative contracts across the world to be $680 trillion, up from $106 trillion in 2002 and a relative pittance just two decades ago. Theoretically intended to limit risk and ward off financial problems, the contracts instead have stoked uncertainty and actually spread risk amid doubts about how companies value them. Derivatives are hard to value. They are virtually hidden from investors, analysts and regulators, even though they are one of Wall Street's biggest profit engines. They do not trade openly on public exchanges, and financial services firms disclose few details about them. "[16] Efforts are afoot to create new market institutions such as clearing houses but the underlying problem remains: derivatives create imaginary risks and then multiply the financial transactions beyond recognition from the underlying value of assets, rendering such derivatives to be mere debts or gambling transactions in a clearing house branch of a casino.

"To improve the safety of the financial system, the Dodd-Frank reform law requires that most derivative deals be executed on a clearinghouse that will require traders to post collateral and will provide a central place for regulators to keep an eye on risk in the market. The idea was to increase transparency in a market that played a key role in the financial crisis and led to the federal $182.3 billion bailout of American International Group in 2008."[17]

Two years after the Dodd-Frank recommendations have been in place, some additional reform measures are suggested to arrive at a stable and integrated global financial system:

•Implement the Volcker Rule to protect taxpayers from excessive risk-taking by financial institutions.

• Finalize derivatives reform to protect our markets from overspeculation in this hundred-trillion-dollar market.

13

- Ensure financial regulators have the resources to protect taxpayers by adequately funding the Commodity Futures Trading Commission.

- Hold the line on mortgage origination and securitization to protect homeowners, investors and taxpayers.
- Continue to ensure coordinated global financial reform and strong international minimum capital standards are enacted.[18]

By being allowed to trade in derivatives, banks put their capital at risk. Insurance against risks has itself been made into a risk by the speculating market. When the fence eats away the field, who is to save the crop?

In today's market, the operative techniques are not prices of assets, determined by buyers and sellers, but by irresponsible agencies of hedge funds, leverages, credit-defaul swaps, derivatives. Speculation is the driving force and to make huge profits, hedge funds use leverage to the tune of 20 to 1, that is, for every dollar in assets hedge funds had, investment of $20 was from borrowed money.

"Derivatives massively leverage the debt in an economy, making it ever more difficult for the underlying real economy to service its debt obligations, thereby curtailing real economic activity, which can cause a recession or even depression."[19]

The Dodd–Frank Wall Street Reform and Consumer Protection Act (Pub.L. 111-203, H.R. 4173) was signed into federal law by President Barack Obama on July 21, 2010.[1] Passed as a response to the late-2000s recession, it brought the most significant changes to financial regulation in the United States since the regulatory reform that followed the Great Depression.[20]

[quote] Summary: Restoring American Financial Stability

Create a Sound Economic Foundation to Grow Jobs, Protect Consumers, Rein in Wall Street, End Too Big to Fail, Prevent Another Financial Crisis

Americans have faced the worst financial crisis since the Great Depression. Millions have lost their jobs, businesses have failed, housing prices have dropped, and savings were wiped out.

The failures that led to this crisis require bold action. We must restore responsibility and accountability in our financial system to give Americans confidence that there is a system in place that works for and protects them.

We must create a sound foundation to grow the economy and create jobs.

Highlights of the New Bill

Consumer Protections with Authority and Independence: Creates a new independent watchdog, housed at the Federal Reserve, with the authority to ensure American consumers get the clear, accurate information they need to shop for mortgages, credit cards, and other financial products, and protect them from hidden fees, abusive terms, and deceptive practices.

Ends Too Big to Fail Bailouts: Ends the possibility that taxpayers will be asked to write a check to bail out financial firms that threaten the economy by: creating a safe way to liquidate failed financial firms; imposing tough new capital and leverage requirements that make it undesirable to get too big; updating the Fed's authority to allow system-wide support but no longer prop up individual firms; and establishing rigorous standards and supervision to protect the economy and American consumers, investors and businesses.

Advance Warning System: Creates a council to identify and address systemic risks posed by large, complex companies, products, and activities before they threaten the stability of the economy.

Transparency & Accountability for Exotic Instruments: Eliminates loopholes that allow risky and abusive practices to go on unnoticed and unregulated - including loopholes for over-the-counter derivatives, assetbacked securities, hedge funds, mortgage brokers and payday lenders.

Federal Bank Supervision: Streamlines bank supervision to create clarity and accountability. Protects the dual banking system that supports community banks.

Executive Compensation and Corporate Governance: Provides shareholders with a say on pay and corporate affairs with a non-binding vote on executive compensation.

Protects Investors: Provides tough new rules for transparency and accountability for credit rating agencies to protect investors and businesses.

Enforces Regulations on the Books: Strengthens oversight and empowers regulators to aggressively pursue financial fraud, conflicts of interest and manipulation of the system that benefit special interests at the expense of American families and businesses. [unquote][21]

Whether the 'reform' will deliver is a moot question and some believe that the attempt will be a failure leaving the ban on derivatives as a rational option. This possibility is elaborated in the context of attempts at competitive mortgage securitization attempted during the 1880s, the 1920s and the 2000s: "U.S. policymakers often treat market competition as a panacea. However, in the case of mortgage securitization, policymakers' faith in competition is misplaced. Competitive mortgage securitization has been tried three times in U.S. history - during the 1880s, the 1920s, and the 2000s - and every time it has failed. Most recently, competition between mortgage securitizers led to a race to the bottom on mortgage underwriting standards that ended in the late 2000s financial crisis. This article provides original evidence that when competition was less intense and securitizers had more market power, securitizers acted to monitor mortgage originators and to maintain prudent underwriting. However, securitizers' ability to monitor originators and maintain high standards was undermined as competition shifted market power away from securitizers and toward originators. Although standards declined across the market, the largest and most powerful of the mortgage securitizers, the Government Sponsored Enterprises ("GSEs"), remained more successful than other mortgage securitizers at maintaining prudent underwriting. This article proposes reforms based on lessons from the recent financial crisis: merge the GSEs with various government agencies' mortgage operations to create a single dedicated mortgage securitization agency that would seek to maintain market stability, improve underwriting, and provide a long term investment return for the benefit of taxpayers."[22]

GDP share of US Financial Industry

Source: Philippon, 2008

18

Share in <u>GDP</u> of U.S. financial sector since 1860[23]

Derivatives (financial instruments as fictional statements, built without underlying assets) were the root cause of the mortgage crisis USA faced. Credit-default swaps (a way of buying insurance against your neighbor's house catching fire, a way of speculating on sovereign debt) bought from American International Group led to the collapse of Lehman Brothers. The investment bank's bond ratings got lowered when stock prices fell and credit-default swaps rose in price. Lower credit ratings meant a downturn in the price of Lehman's stock. This vicious cycle drove Lehman Brothers out of business.

Speculation. One example is shorting of shares -- the practice of borrowing a share expected to fall and selling it, hoping to buy it back later at a lower price, pocketing the difference.

"Derivatives are bets between two parties that are made today with a payoff in the future based on the value of some stock, bond, or index. One party will profit if the reference security or index goes up in value and the other party will profit if it goes down. These bets usually settle up every three months based on value at that time, and then a new calculation period begins. There are many variations on this basic pattern, but almost all derivatives involve some form of a bet in which gains and losses are calculated and settled-up periodically." Simply, derivatives become instruments in the hands of speculators to manipulate markets.[24]

Derivatis do not improve price discovery. Unlike bonds which are widely held by a large number of investors, credit-default swaps are tightly controlled by a small number of major bank dealers who set prices in a nontransparent way. Such swaps are thus easier to manipulate than the underlying bond market. Derivatives simply make the market manipulation by speculators easier.

Unless hedge funds, derivatives, credit-default swaps are banned, markets will continue to dictate the fate of capitalists and communists alike, driven by speculation which is another name for greed. One estimate is that just 9 big banks have a derivative exposure of $228.72 trillion. This is indicative of the enormous risks created by the financial system which is destined to undergo the cycles of booms and busts.[25]

With such bizarre techniques developed with the assistance of nerds from such institutions as MIT, the market has bloated beyond recognition., beyond any conceivable faor valuation of underlying assets.

'In the money' is a poker term used to finish high enough in a poker tournament to win prize money. In the context of financial derivatives which have engulfed the market and the globe, this is explained as 'moneyness'. "In finance, moneyness is the relative position of the current price (or future price) of an underlying asset (e.g., a stock) with respect to the strike price of a derivative, most commonly a call option or a put option. Moneyness is firstly a three-fold classification: if the derivative would make money if it were to expire today, it is said to be in the money, while if it would not make money it is said to be out of the money, and if the current price and strike price are equal, it is said to be at the money. There are two slightly different definitions, according to whether one uses the current price (spot) or future price (forward), specified as "at the money spot" or "at the money forward", etc. This rough classification can be quantified by various definitions to express the moneyness as a number, measuring how far the asset is in the money or out of the money with respect to the strike – or conversely how far a strike is in or out of the money with respect to the spot (or forward) price of the asset. This quantified notion of moneyness is most importantly used in defining the relative volatility surface: the implied volatility in terms of moneyness, rather than absolute price. The most basic of these measures is simple moneyness, which is the ratio of spot (or forward) to strike, or the reciprocal, depending on convention. A particularly important measure of moneyness is the likelihood that the derivative will expire in the money, in the risk-neutral measure. It can be measured in percentage probability of expiring in the money, which is the forward value of a binary option with the given strike. This can also be measured in standard deviations, measuring how far above or below the strike price the current price is, in terms of volatility. Another closely related measure of moneyness is the Delta of a call or put option, which is often used by traders, and there are others... Moneyness can be defined mathematically using the Black–Scholes model, by using the model to compute an implied volatility from the current price of the option. One then uses this volatility, together with the risk-free rate, to define the risk-neutral measure, and then defines the moneyness with respect to this measure. One generally defines the forward moneyness (moneyness with respect to the forward price), as this corresponds to "likelihood of expiring in the money". The moneyness (in standard deviations) is defined as:

$$m = \frac{\ln\left(F/K\right)}{\sigma\sqrt{\tau}} = \frac{\ln(S/K) + rT}{\sigma\sqrt{T}},$$

where F is the forward price of the underlying, K is the strike price, σ is the implied volatility, and τ is the time to expiry; the alternative formula uses the strike price S and the risk-free rate r. All of these are observables except for the implied volatility, which is computed from the observable price using the Black–Scholes formula. In words, the moneyness is the number of standard deviations the current forward price is above the strike price. Thus the moneyness is zero when the forward price of the underlying equals the strike price, when the option is at-the-money-forward. Moneyness is measured in standard deviations from this point, with a positive value meaning an in-the-money call option and a negative value meaning an out-of-the-money call option (with signs reversed for a put option)... Derivatives can be used for speculation ("bets") or to hedge ("insurance"). For example, a speculator may sell deep in-the-money naked calls on a stock, expecting the stock price to plummet, but exposing himself to potentially unlimited losses."[26]

What the nerds have ended up creating is best evidenced by "Stock market & world GDP statistical data sculptures" shown below.

"The wooden data sculpture titled Fundament [anfischer.com] compares the allocation of the world's gross domestic product with the worldwide derivatives volume. The piece consists of two layers: the lower half is a mapping of the world's GDP and the top half is a mapping of the derivatives volume, alloted to the coordinates of the countries on a map. In turn, the horizontal arrangement equates to the Mercator projection of a world map and the vertical axis metaphorically corresponds to the financial activity of the country. The statistical data was aquired from the CIA World Factbook and the International Monetary Fund. The data sculpture Indizes [anfischer.com] visualizes the stock market indices S & P 500, Dow Jones Industrial and NASDAQ in the year 2008 from January to November. The values are shown on the three peaks of the five rows of polygons. The data was provided by Google Finance."[27]

Mapping of the world gross domestic product 2007

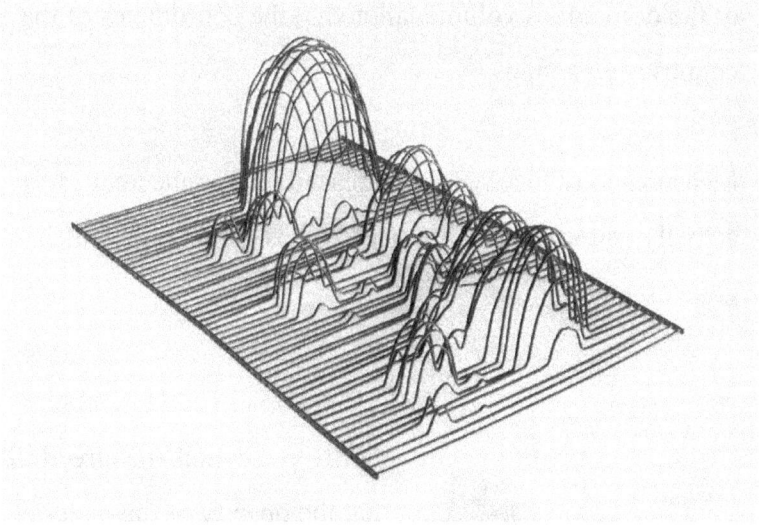

Mapping of the world derivatives volume 2007

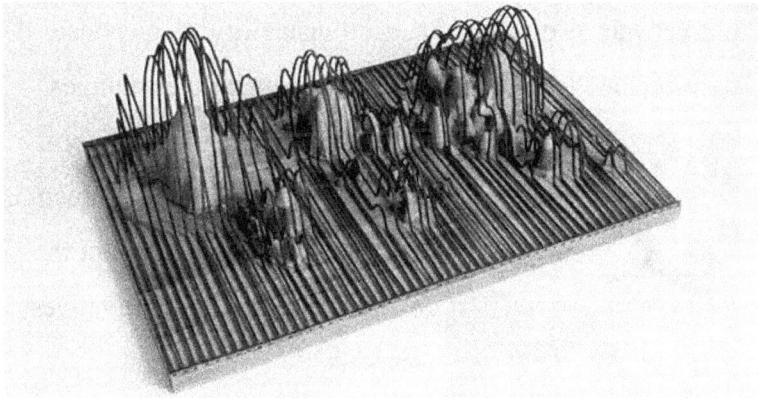

Comparison of the two layers

The piece consists of two layers: the lower half is a
mapping of the world's GDP and the top half is a mapping

of the derivatives volume, alloted to the coordinates of the countries on a map.

Measures to reduce risk of increased interconnectedness actually end up increasing risk. This is gambler's walk gone bizarre.

"AFTER the crisis (in September 2012), policymakers agreed that the opacity of the over-the-counter (OTC) derivatives market was a source of financial instability. In response, they decided to push derivatives trading onto exchanges that would require firms to post safe collateral. But, the problem is not the lack of collateral but the excessive size of the derivatives markets."[28]

Gambler's den. Haves and have-nots? No. Dealers and non-dealers.

" To its detractors, the over-the-counter (OTC) derivatives market is like a rigged poker game. They picture a smoke-filled room, in which unsuspecting clients are mastered by skilful opponents at investment banks known, perhaps appropriately, as dealers."[29]

Derivatives are financial instruments (contracts) that have their value determined by another (financial) product. An option (put or call) in the stock markets is a derivative.

An ancient Greek mathematician and philosopher, Thales of Miletus is mentioned in Aristotle's. Politics. On a certain occasion, it was predicted that the season's olive harvest would be larger than usual, and during the off-season he acquired the right to use a number of olive presses the following spring. When spring came and the olive harvest was larger than expected he exercised his options and then rented the presses out at much higher price than he paid for his 'option'.

Figure 1
Market Capitalisation and GDP in $ Billions

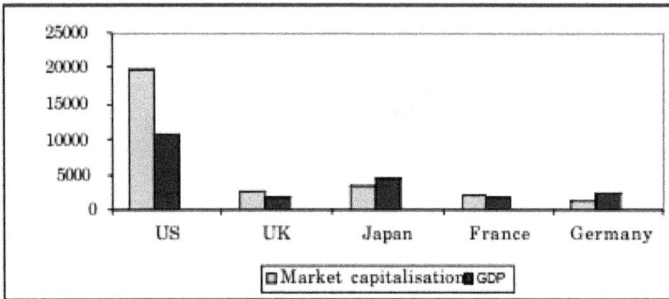

Figure 2
Ratio of Market Capitalisation in Relation to GDP (%)

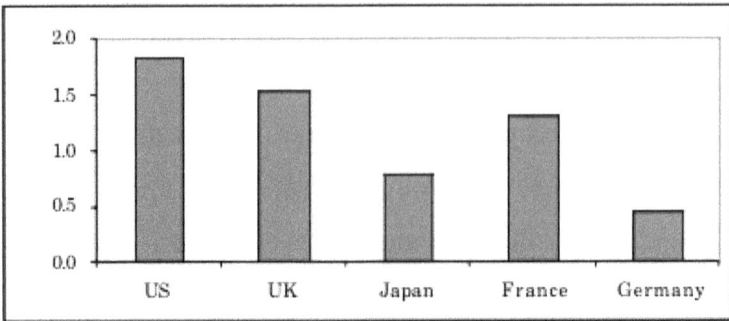

Germany's stock market capitalization is relatively small in relation to the level of economic activity. German stock market is the smallest when compared to the value added generated in the country. Stock price movements have a potentially smaller impact on aggregate household wealth, than is the case in other countries where the ratio of market capitalization to GDP is higher.[30]

Table 1
Top Ten Biggest Stock Markets in the World (% of Total)

No.	Market	%
1	United States	47.6
2	Japan	10.2
3	United Kingdom	10.2
4	France	4.6
5	Canada	3.2
6	Germany	2.9
7	Switzerland	2.9
8	Italy	2.3
9	Australia	2.0
10	Netherlands	2.0

Source: Wren Research, June 2005

Country	Market Cap / GDP	Market Cap ($mn)	GDP ($mn)	Market type
Italy	0.30	604,901	2,036,687	Developed
Netherlands	0.43	327,604	770,312	Developed
Turkey	0.43	310,996	729,051	Emerging
Germany	0.46	1,515,063	3,305,898	Developed
Spain	0.46	630,181	1,374,779	Developed
Russia	0.47	691,005	1,476,912	Emerging
Mexico	0.50	500,097	1,004,042	Emerging
Indonesia	0.52	361,820	695,059	Emerging
Belgium	0.59	272,845	461,331	Developed
China	0.66	3,813,920	5,745,133	Emerging
Norway	0.70	289,029	413,511	Developed
France	0.70	1,796,545	2,555,439	Developed
Brazil	0.72	1,457,790	2,023,528	Emerging
Japan	0.74	4,013,490	5,390,897	Developed
Canada	0.76	1,193,428	1,563,664	Developed
Saudi Arabia	0.83	358,730	434,440	Emerging
Thailand	0.89	277,345	312,605	Emerging
United States	1.06	15,559,765	14,624,184	Developed
South Korea	1.11	1,098,158	986,256	Developed
India	1.14	1,628,673	1,430,020	Emerging
Australia	1.20	1,463,179	1,219,722	Developed
Sweden	1.36	604,253	444,585	Developed
United Kingdom	1.50	3,389,874	2,258,565	Developed
South Africa	1.50	532,890	354,414	Emerging
Chile	1.67	331,719	199,183	Emerging
Malaysia	1.89	413,515	218,950	Emerging
Taiwan	2.16	921,883	426,984	Emerging
Switzerland	2.28	1,193,428	522,435	Developed
Singapore	2.70	586,722	217,377	Developed

Compiled by Ox Mountain Financial Jan 2011

Source of GDP: International Monetary Fund 2010[31]

"By simply dividing each country's stock market capitalization by its GDP, I was able to generate the bubble graph below. The size of the bubble indicates the size of the market cap but the key here is the Market Cap to GDP ratio as measured by the y axis."[32]

Market capitalization of listed companies (% of GDP) in world

The Market capitalization of listed companies (% of GDP) in World was last reported at 66.29 in 2011, according to a World Bank report published in 2012. Market capitalization (also known as market value) is the share price times the number of shares outstanding. Listed domestic companies are the domestically incorporated companies listed on the country's stock exchanges at the end of the year. Listed companies does not include investment companies, mutual funds, or other collective investment vehicles.This page includes a historical data chart, news and forecasts for Market capitalization of listed companies (% of GDP) in World.

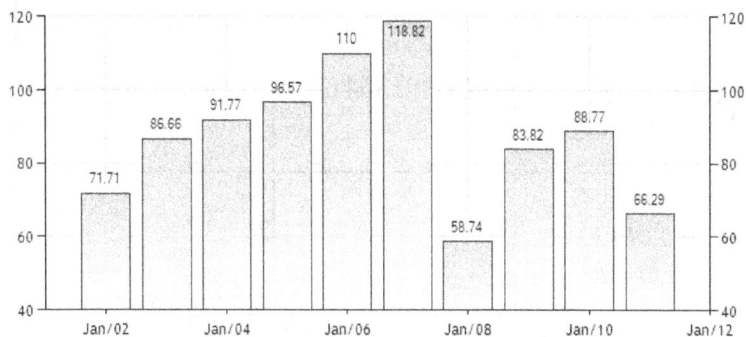

31

World bank indicators – World Capital markets[33]

	Previous (Jan/06)	Last (Jan/08)
Listed domestic companies; total in World	51388.0	49692.0
Market capitalization of listed companies (% of GDP) in World	118.8	58.7
Market capitalization of listed companies (US dollar) in World	64575372716978.7	34900892787655.3
Stocks traded; total value (% of GDP) in World	181.9	181.8
Stocks traded; total value (US dollar) in World	98816391364122.4	108066332046301.0
Stocks traded; turnover ratio (%) in World	167.6	217.3

The myth of GDP and Stock Market Returns[34]

Economists spend a great deal of time thinking about GDP growth rates in various countries around the world and investors often consider these forecasts when deciding where to put their money. Common wisdom is that countries with strong long-term economic growth prospects are more likely to provide attractive stock market returns than countries with slower growth expectations. Interestingly enough, the historical data does not back up this belief.

Chart 1

Dimson, Marsh, and Staunton's *Triumph of the Optimists: 101 Years of Global Investment Returns* includes stock market returns from 1900 to 2000 for 16 developed countries. The data clearly shows that, over long periods and when adjusted for inflation, stock market returns and GDP per capita growth are negatively correlated. The data was updated through 2002 by Professor Jay Ritter in his paper, *Economic Growth and Equity Returns*. As Chart 1 shows, at best, there is no relationship between GDP per capita and stock returns over the long term.

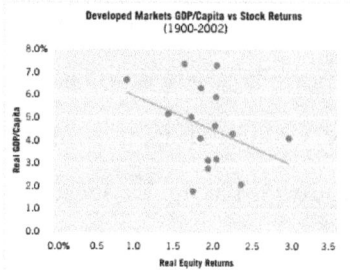

Developed Markets GDP/Capita vs Stock Returns (1900-2002)

Source: Vontobel Asset Management

"The stock market has called nine out of the last five recessions" – Paul A. Samuelson "If you spend 13 minutes a year trying to predict the economy, you have wasted 10 minutes" – Peter Lynch, stock guru.[35]

Apple's stock market value, or market cap, of $506bn (£323bn) makes it worth more than Poland, whose Gross Domestic Product is about $470bn (£300bn). Is Apple really worth more than Poland or, really the 20th biggest economy in the world?

"There is another respectable way to compare the two. For this, calculate Apple's "added value" and compare that to Poland's GDP. (The Financial Times' business glossary defines added value as "an increase in the value of something that has been worked on, so that it can be sold in a new form".) This makes sense because GDP is essentially a measure of a country's added value - it is the value of all the goods and services there, minus anything that has been imported. "We would take the sales of Apple and subtract everything that is in the iPhone, but that Apple has not produced itself," De Grauwe says. "For example, some chips, or the screen, which has been produced in China somewhere. And the difference then is what you could call the value added by Apple. And that we compare with GDP which is the value added in Poland."[36]

Global crisis and the decline of market fundamentalist form of capitalism

Joseph Stiglitz calls the approach taken since the 1980s by the World Bank and IMF as 'market fundamentalism', a re-affirmation of a belief system that laissez-faire of free markets, 'capital-account liberalization' (or removal of barriers to enable flow of capital into and out of countries), in particular, resolves economic problems. Stiglitz identifies this as the single factor influenced by Wall Street, which contributed to the global economic crisis of 1990's. (Joseph Stiglitz, 2002, Globalization and its discontents, New York, WW Norton & Company)

Kenneth Rogoff, IMF Director of Research referred to Stiglitz's analysis as 'snake oil' and added: "The Stiglitzian prescription (for third world nations in a debt crisis) is to raise the profile of fiscal deficits, that is, to issue more debt and to print more money. You seem to believe that if a distressed government issues more currency, its citizens will suddenly think it more valuable.

You seem to believe that when investors are no longer willing to hold a government's debt, all that needs to be done is to increase the supply and it will sell like hot cakes…(Rogoff concluded): Throughout your book, you betray an unrelenting belief in the pervasiveness of market failures, and a staunch conviction that governments can and will make things better. You call us "market fundamentalists." We do not believe that markets are always perfect, as you accuse. But we do believe there are many instances of government failure as well and that, on the whole, government failure is a far bigger problem than market failure in the developing world...Joe, as an academic, you are a towering genius. Like your fellow Nobel Prize winner, John Nash, you have a "beautiful mind." As a policymaker, however, you were just a bit less impressive."[37]

Describing Washington consensus policy of free markets as a blend of ideology and bad science, Stiglitz notes: "Behind the free market ideology there is a model, often attributed to <u>Adam Smith</u>, which argues that market forces—the <u>profit</u>motive—drive the economy to efficient outcomes as if by an invisible hand. One of the great achievements of modern economics is to show the sense in which, and the conditions under which, Smith's conclusion is correct. It turns out that these conditions are highly restrictive. Indeed, more recent advances in economic theory—ironically occurring precisely during the period of the most relentless pursuit of the Washington Consensus policies—have shown that whenever information is imperfect and markets incomplete, which is to say always, and especially in developing countries, then the invisible hand works most imperfectly. Significantly, there are desirable government interventions which, in principle, can improve upon the efficiency of the market. These restrictions on the conditions under which markets result in efficiency are important—many of the key activities of government can be understood as responses to the resulting market failures." (Note: An imperfect market[38] is a market where information is not quickly disclosed to all participants in it and where the matching of buyers and sellers isn't immediate.)

Without equal access to information, markets cannot be 'free' and 'fair'.

The liberalization hides the nature of the money which flows. It is speculative hot money flowing into gullible developing markets evidenced by the devaluation of Thai baht in 1997 caused by pull out of such money shattering investor confidence and resultant upto ten-fold increase in unemployment in some national economies.

Rumen Georgiev of Sofia University provides an overview on the decline of market fundamentalism and the resurgence of state interventions to cope with the global financial crisis caused by excessive debts and speculative activities using financial derivatives:

[quote]The structural deformation of US economy and society, ensuing from â€œmarket fundamentalismâ€ and â€œmonetaristic rideâ€ of scientific and technical innovations, can be clearly demonstrated by the following facts and indicators:

- The total amount of unpaid credits, excluding the widely used derivative financial instruments, in the US in 2008 reached 365% of the GDP (compared to 250% in 1932) [2, p.123];
- The ratio between the indicators for the average annual profit growth and the private sector salary levels has deteriorated dramatically: for the period 2000 â€“ 2007 it

was 8.2% to 1 %, while for the period 1979 â€" 1990 it was 2.6% to 1.7% [9];

- Profits of the financial sector as percentage of the aggregate profit of all US corporations increased from 14% in 1981 to 39% in 2001 and to about 50% in 2007 [8, p.10];
- Household debts as percentage of the available personal incomes skyrocketed from 66% in 1980 to 91.1% in 2000 and to 128.8% in 2007. The actual median household income, which reflects business activity (and to some extent the actual potential for solvent consumer demand as well), dropped in 2007 below the level of 2000 [10];
- The overall amount of US debt skyrocketed as well and as of 2008 it exceeded USD 50 trillion or 90% of the world GDP. The Federal Government debt for the period 2000 â€" 2008 ballooned from USD 5.7 trillion to USD 10.7 trillion. The major holders of US Treasury Securities as of the beginning of the crisis are China (USD 653 billion), Japan (USD 585 billion) and oil exporters [11]. Thus, the global imbalances in the international capital flows reached critical limits, the attractiveness of US dollar as reserve currency dwindled and it became necessary to develop quickly the domestic consumption in countries with capital surplus (above all China).

Under these cicrumstances, the measures, undertaken by the USA and most other countries in the world after 2007 â€" 2008, no matter how diverse they were, naturally focused upon a painstaking government monetary intervention in the financial institutions â€" banks, mortgage agencies, insurance companies, etc. If such a powerful government support had not been provided, then the financial and banking systems in most countries worldwide would have crashed long ago, triggering even worse consequences for themselves than the ones in 1929 â€" 1933…

The threats to the sustainability and the further development of world economy, including the economies of the US and the other economic leaders, had a great impact over G20 member countries which as early as November 2008 adopted an unprecedented for the period of â€œmarket fundamentalismâ€• Declaration Summit on Financial Markets and the World Economy. It states the common will of the countries to unite their efforts to correct the actions of market forces and promote the role of the governments in the new spheres of activity, generated by the scientific and technical progress. It would be inaccurate to quote one section or another of the systematically elaborated Declaration as this would distort its integral meaning â€"what really matters is that the envisaged actions should be implemented. It would not be exaggerated to state that the elaboration of this Declaration and the decisions adopted at subsequent G-20 summits testify not so much to the overruling of pragmatism over liberalism but to the fact that we witness the laying of the foundations for the development of a new economic paradigm of the 21st century. The starting point of the planned actions is the sustainability of world economy and the stable development of national economies as guarantees for civil rights and freedoms. National interests define the way private interests are to be safeguarded. The more markets, the greater the need for regulation on the part of the governments and the larger their responsibility for the vectors of economic and social development of countries and regions. ..

[One of the activity directions for consideration] - There are propositions for the establishment of clearer and more transparent rules for the regulation of complex (secondary) financial instruments through the establishment of controlled hubs, which could be clearing houses for example, to perform stock trading. This will affect above all the credit swaps market. Meanwhile, the need of additional taxes on particular speculative deals is frequently discussed...

- Measures for the enhanced coordination between budget and fiscal policy with the banking and monetary policy in regional and national aspects are under way . Further proof of that is the stronger effort and intensive actions for the implementation of rules for long-term financial sustainability on national and regional association level (such as â€œpactsâ€• , â€œboardsâ€• , etc.). Under the current instability, though, these could only be successful if they ensure not only better budget discipline in annual terms, but also a better business climate and investment activity, which are necessary in the long-term.   [unquote][39]

Network of corporate control of economic activity in the globe

John Maynard Keynes wrote his essay, 'The End of Laissez-faire' in 1926. little did he realize the economic history through two millennia had impoverished a third of the globe. His economic theory faced the shocks of the Great Depression which further unraveled through hot and cold wars, the rise of global market fundamentalism, dethroning of the gold standard, oil shocks, rise of technological innovations in medicine and communications. Nor did Keynes offer any solutions to restore the third of the globe to its rightful share of the wealth of nations.

The history of existing societies is a history of denial of individual identity and freedom, a history of denial of social responsibility. The result is promotion of corporate domination and increased corporate greed.

The same Keynes had in 1919 published his essay, "The Economic Consequences of the Peace" noted that British people witnessed globalization as "normal, certain and permanent, except in the direction of further improvement and any deviation from it as aberrant, scandalous and avoidable." Little did Keynes realize that 'laissez-faire' economics coupled with globalization resulted in the impoverishment of a third of the globe through colonial loots of unprecedented magnitudes, camouflaging 'imperialist' diktats as 'globalization' as a natural extension of 'laissez-faire'.

Will the temporary victory of the markets in 1913 over political economy and the power of the state to render social justice be repeated in the wake of market fundamentalism of the 21st century? George Soros says no: "I argue that the current state of affairs is unsound and unsustainable. Financial markets are inherently unstable and there are social needs that cannot be met by giving market forces free rein. It is market fundamentalism that has rendered the global capitalistic system unsound and unsustainable. This is a relatively recent state of affairs. At the end of the Second World War, the international movement of capital was restricted and Bretton woods institutions were set up to facilitate trade in the absence of capital movements. Restrictions were removed only gradually, and it was only when Margaret Thatcher and

Ronald Reagan came to power around 1980 that market fundamentalism become the dominant ideology."

After the oil shocks of the 1970s, Kissinger's intervention making the dollar as the currency for oil prices has resulted in phenomenal rise in international capital movements and consequent declaration of the markets – London and New York financial markets, in particular -- as the centerpieces of global capitalism.[40] The dominance of market fundamentalism and foreign exchange crises triggered and manipulated by the financial markets was evidenced in the financial crises of the Tiger economies[41] of Asia in 1990's, principally caused by withdrawal of private capital flows from the rich markets to these economies. The value of Thai currency was slashed in half and 56 of the 58 Thai finance companies went bankrupt. The Ruble crisis of August 1998 resulting in devaluation of the ruble and Russis defaulting on its debt, was also caused by market fundamentalism absorbing the largely-barter economy of Russia into the global financial juggernaut.[42]

"300 Years of Stock Market Manipulations – From the Coffeehouse to the World Wide Web's Stock Manipulations...As information technology has expanded the scope of resources available to legitimate investors and traders, the Web has also become the prime new venue for the old game of market manipulation. Institutional traders and other long-term market participants often comment that they see far more inexplicable price moves than they did in the pre-Web era. In many cases, these moves are tied to subtle, and not so subtle, attempts at market manipulation using the newfound power of the Internet to transmit and spread rumors, manipulate beliefs, and post incorrect information at little cost, while maintaining the cloak of anonymity. Price distortions arising from manipulations may be short-lived, but they are real prices, and can dramatically affect the cost of trading and investment performance. The influence of the rumor machine is overlaid on the influences of more fundamental (and benign) factors that move stock prices. Therefore, interest in manipulations is not confined to the most obvious potential victims, specialists, dealers, and market makers but to all buy-side traders."[43]

We have today, a *de facto* US dollar standard since the 1970s. The dominance of Pax Americana can be reversed by strengthening regional communities such as the

European Community[44], since 1957 and the emerging Indian Ocean Community of the 21st century.

What was sought to be created was a Common Market. The Council of European Union with a common Court, Parliament and Commission had limited inputs. While a customs union, common policies for agriculture, transport and trade were adopted together with a common currency called the Euro, the Federation of European Securities Exchanges[45] notes the absence of involvement by Small and Medium-sized Enterprises in the market activities. Of the 20 million SMEs in Europe, only several thousand are listed on exchanges.[46] The importance of SMEs in Euro economy may be gauged from the following table for 2012[47]:

Table 2.1 Number of enterprises, employment and gross value added in EU-27, by size-class, 2012 (estimates)

	Micro	Small	Medium	SMEs	Large	Total
Number of enterprises						
Number	19,143,521	1,357,533	226,573	20,727,627	43,654	20,771,281
%	92.2	6.5	1.1	99.8	0.2	100
Employment						
Number	38395819	26771287	22310205	87477311	42318854	129796165
%	29.6	20.6	17.2	67.4	32.6	100
Gross value added						
EUR Millions	1307360.7	1143935.7	1136243.5	3587540	2591731.5	6179271.4
%	21.2	18.5	18.4	58.1	41.9	100

Source: Eurostat/National Statistics Offices of Member States/Cambridge Econometrics/Ecorys

The economy of the European Union had a Gross Domestic Product in 2011 of over 17.578 trillion, the largest economy in the world, but with public debt accounting for 82.5% of GDP, uemployment of 10.7% and 17% of population below poverty threshold[48]. Imports and exports in 2011, respectively accounted for 1.683 trillion euro and 1.531 trillion euro, rendering the economy of European Community essentially self-reliant. Within the European Community, Germany accounted for 2.570 trillion of 2011 GDP (14.62%) and labor force of 43.62 million. Allianz, a German multinational financial services company based in Munich was the 12th largest financial services group as of 2010 and had 1.443 trillion euro of assets under management.

The value added by Large enterprises was 25,917,731 euro (providing employment to 42,318,854 workers) compared with SMEs contribution of only 3,587,540

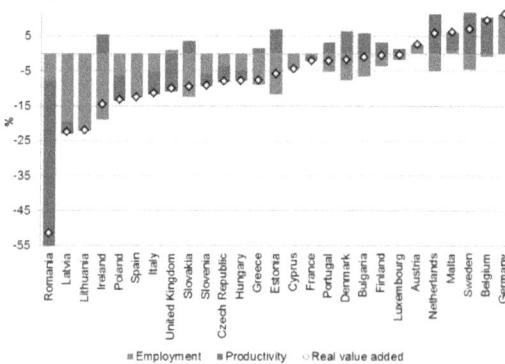

Figure 2.13 Annual growth percentages in employment, real value added and real productivity of SMEs in EU27, 2008-2011

■ Employment ■ Productivity ◇ Real value added

Source: Euroslat/National Statistics Offices of Member States/Cambridge Econometrics/Ecorys

48

euro, while providing employment to 87,477,311 workers. The dismal economic portrait for the years 2008-2011 is seen across almost all 27 countries of European Community with the exception of Germany: The answer to overcome the dismal state of political economy is a wordy recommendation of : "...a need for developing a best-practice incubation model designed for spin-offs in high-tech and medium high-tech manufacturing and knowledge-intensive services." This is, in effect, admission of failure of the European Community economic model, counterbalanced by the limited penetration of market fundamentalism in European community.

This lopsided portrait of European Community economy compares with the lopsided situation in Indian Ocean Community.

As Dani Rodrik noted: "Polanyi's enduring insight is that markets are sustainable only insofar as they are embedded in social and political institutions. The institutions serve three functions without which markets cannot survive: they regulate, stabilize, and legitimate market outcomes. This is why every functioning society has regulatory bodies that prevent unfair competition and fraud, monetary and fiscal institutions that help smooth out the boom-bust cycle as well as social insurance schemes that help bring market outcomes into conformity with a society's preference regarding the distribution of risks and rewards."[49] We simply do not have global institutions to supervise financial markets to make them respond to the social imperative of combating greed and promoting local initiatives and innovations in societies across the globe. Global capitalism of cross-border transactions has to be tempered by federations of communities coordinating state interventions to harmonise with the prescriptions rendered as international rules by agencies such as the World Bank of IMF. Monolithic ideology of market fundamentalism as an extension of laissez-faire should yield place to federating state structures and dialogues with the operatives who can exercise the state power to regulate the imperfections of the financial markets.

Jurgen Habermas[50] rejected postmodernism which reduced innovative thought to an aesthetic experience excluding practical and pure reason from its scope. This is a call for an economic theory of justice. "Specifically, the idea of being 'modern' by looking back to the ancients changed with the belief, inspired by modern science, in the infinite progress of knowledge and in the infinite advance towards social and moral betterment," noted Habermas.

Keynes might have tried to explain away the busts and booms inherent, as a fundamental characteristic, in market fundamentalism, glibly claiming that "many of the greatest economics evils of our time are fruits of risk, uncertainty, and ignorance". Such a statement merely hides the fact that market auctioneers astutely justify the speculations led by greed, as hedging with little concern for the economic and social chaos they wreak on the colonially-looted economies.

The network corporate[51]

Trans-national corporations (TNC) "[...] comprise companies and other entities established in more than one country and so linked that they may coordinate their operations in various ways, while one or more of these entities may be able to exercise a significant influence over the activities of others, their degree of autonomy within the enterprise may vary widely from one multinational enterprise to another. Ownership may be private, state or mixed."[52]

From a list of 43060 TNCs identified according to the definition, the team, led by S. Vitali of the Swiss Federal Institute of Technology in Zurich, used a method of analysis often applied to connectivity in the internet. Called the "bow-tie model," the method assigns companies onto the parts of a bow-tie. They find that a few TNCs are seen to control fully 40% of the economic value of TNCs: 4/10 of the control over the economic value of TNCs in the world is held, via a complicated web of ownership relations, by a group of 147 TNCs in the core, which has almost full control over itself.[53]

 "We find that transnational corporations form a giant bow-tie structure and that a large portion of control flows to a small tightly-knit core of financial institutions. This core can be seen as an economic "super-entity" that raises new important issues both for researchers and policy makers." A "super-entity" of 147 companies, or 0.3% of all TNCs, holds control over fully 40% of the economic value of TNCs.

 Some major TNCs in the financial sector are identified in the network of corporates.

Inter-connected companies sit on the knot of the bow tie shape. All of the companies in the knot have control

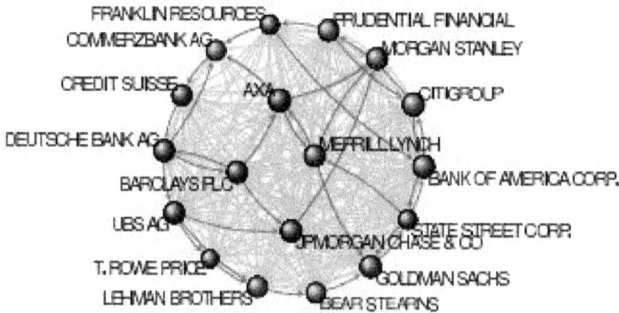

relationships to other companies in the knot and are themselves controlled by other companies in the knot. Companies which control those in the knot, but are not themselves controlled in return, are visualized on one wing of the bow-tie. And companies controlled by those in the knot, but not themselves controlling, are on the other wing of the bowtie.

The fact that a small number of companies are highly connected in the knot does not prove unbalanced control; after all, it is normal in networking that everyone wants a connection to the powerful few, who connect out to those who can offer something in return. But by combining the bow-tie topology with a control ranking, the team came to an amazing conclusion.

Less than 1% of Companies in Control

The team found a core of 1318 companies (mostly financial services companies) with an average of 20 control links each amongst themselves. These 1318 companies represent only 0.7% of the TNCs but 18.7% of the revenue of all TNCs. When one adds in the 59.8% of the revenues from companies on the wing of the bow-tie controlled by those in the knot, these companies control almost 80% of the global economy.

A just economy is premised on goodness, fairness, and justice, generally in close-knot communities operating as social networks.In "The Moral Economy of the Crowd" Thompson states his theory: "It is possible to detect in almost ever eighteenth-century crowd action some legitimising notion. By the notion of legitimation I mean that the men and women in the crowd were informed by the belief that they were defending traditional rights or customs; and, in general, that they were supported by the wider consensus of the community. On occasion this popular consensus was endorsed by some measure of licence afforded by the authorities. More commonly, the consensus was so strong that it overrode motives of fear or deference."[54]

The Great Depression of the 1930's and the Global Financial Crisis of 2000's highlight the flaws of unrestrained markets and bankers creating inflation and contraction in money supply, resulting in cycles of boom and bust. In what is referred to as 'neo-liberalism', John Maynard Keynes offered an economic management solution to these cycles, by direct ownership or regulated private ownership, deficit spending during contraction and budget surpluses during inflation. The consequence was creation of classes of elites and depressed.

Market fundamentalism is an economic or political doctrinaire term used to aver that all problems in society are solved when economic policy is used to 'stabilise, liberalise and privatise'[55] and that unregulated markets will somehow always produce the best possible results for an economy. Market is viewed as a means to resolve differences among constituents in a society on expansion or rollback of social services.

Market fundamentalism is premised on four postultes: 1. Minimum regulation; 2. Regulation is wasteful; 3. Government is the problem, not the solution; an inefficien spender of money; 4. Market is the source of innovation

Economic theories which support government regulation or intervention recount the following facets of economic history:

- Systematic policies by England's government from the 16th to the 18th century to build up the textile industry worked to make England the first industrial nation.

- Canal and railroad building by state and Federal government in the U.S. in the 19thcentury established a foundation for a continental economy.

- A mix of government policies led to rapid economic growth in Japan, Taiwan, and South Korea from the 1950's to the 1980's.

- The current Chinese government's massive investments in education, science, and technology have driven that nation's rapid growth.[56]

Kozul-Wright states in his book that "ineluctability of market forces" neo-liberals and conservative politicians tend to stress, and their confidence on a chosen policy, rest on a "mixture of implicit and hidden assumptions, myths about the history of their own countries' economic development, and special interests camouflaged in their rhetoric of general good"[57]

Market fundamentalism raises the deepest questions about goals of life and pursui of happiness in a human civilization.

Global capitalism attempts to make society subservient

Market fundamentalism has resulted in upsetting the state apple-cart. As Karl Polonyi had noted, in the 1940s, 'instead of the economy being embedded in social relatios, social relations are embedded in the economic system,' in the laisse-faire regime of the 19th century, in its new avatar of 21st century, as market fundamentalism. "Since society was made to conform to the needs of the market mechanism, imperfections in the functioning of that mechanism created cumulative strains on the body social."

Today, the corporation is in league with the state power to impoverish the individuals and to interfere in their life activities.

Corporation has engulfed almost all life activities from the cradle to managing funerals, from prayers in temples to issuance of financial derivatives to replace wealth producing assets.

Eisuke Sakakibara argues eloquently against prescriptions dictated by market fundamentalism: "The blind application of the universal model, be it neo-classical or monetarist, on emerging economies seems to have been the predominant practice by international institutions or other public and private creditors. To some extent, emerging economies themselves accepted such unilateral imposition of dogmatic formulas fearing a negative reaction from the market if they rejected such prescriptions. In this sense, the "Washington" consensus was not only the consensus in Washington but represented the official position of G-7 and other IMF-World Bank member countries, creditors as well as debtors, and market participants. This perfect coordination, on the other hand, generated mutually reinforcing excessively optimistic and then pessimistic expectations about the country in question. The Asian crisis seems to be a good example of this Washington generated excessive optimism turned into panic. Asia, particularly South East Asia, in some sense, was an area well suited for global laissez-faire type financial and commercial transactions. South East Asia had been resonating with Washington-led globalization with their own traditional structure of global commercialism. Between the 8th and 18th centuries, Asia was the center of world commercial activities among Islamic, Indian, and Chinese merchants and later with Venetian, Dutch, and English merchants. Thus, the human networks for global transactions, both financial and commercial, were there and overseas Chinese and Indians could speedily adapt to newly emerging global markets. However, after the Asian crisis, we came to recognize that this resonance of Asian tradition with the Washington consensus had some serious problems. To the extent that markets believed the payoffs for implementing the Washington consensus in Asia were high, Asia euphoria continued and resulted in huge inflows of capital during 1993 to 1996. n One major aspect of the combination of Asian commercialism and financial and telecommunication globalism was that it tended to skim over the surface of economic structures and weakened the manufacturing base. Projects tended to be concentrated in the services and real estate industries, such as the construction of financial centers, rather than basic infrastructure or manufacturing. Thus, education and on-the-job training of workers or organizational improvements in corporations tended to lag behind. Thus, as has been pointed out by many, including Paul Krugman, labor productivity and efficiency gains were not noticeable even in export industries which was affected by the appreciation of the real effective exchange rate. One-time gains in competitiveness due to low wages quickly dissipated, and sky rocketing costs for business offices also resulted in loss in relative competitiveness. Thus, it is fair to say that the Asian crisis was not necessarily generated by the unilateral imposition of the Washington consensus from institutions in Washington but was a result of worldwide euphoria about the market mechanism, including that of Asian countries, that created the bubble and eventually the bursting of bubbles in this region."[58]

Economic history of two millennia

In a breath-taking analysis, Angus Maddison surveys the entire world economy over the past two thousand years, marking changes over time and between regions.

John Maynard Keyes had an advice to a master economist

A history of world GDP
Percentage of total, 1990 $ at PPP*

China · India · Japan · US · France · Germany · Italy · Britain

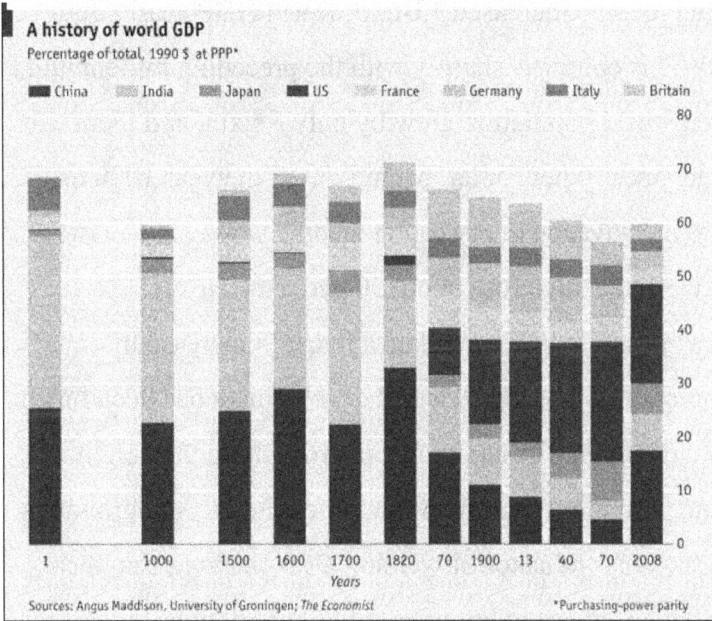

Years: 1 · 1000 · 1500 · 1600 · 1700 · 1820 · 70 · 1900 · 13 · 40 · 70 · 2008

Sources: Angus Maddison, University of Groningen; *The Economist*   *Purchasing-power parity

that he should 'examine the present in light of the past, for the purposes of the future'.

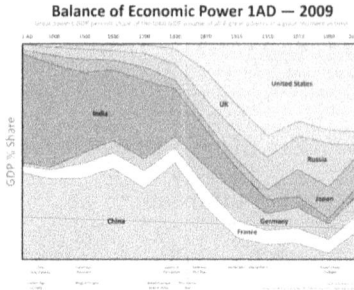

Balance of Economic Power 1AD — 2009

Angus Maddison's survey can be summarized in his own words:

[quote] The contours of World development. Over the past millennium, world population rose 22-fold. Per capita income increased 13-fold, world GDP nearly 300-fold. This contrasts sharply with the preceding millennium, when world population grew by only a sixth, and there was no advance in per capita income. From the year 1000 to 1820 the advance in per capita income was a slow crawl – the world average rose about 50 per cent. Most of the growth went to accommodate a fourfold increase in population. Since 1820, world development has been much more dynamic. Per capita income rose more than eightfold, population more than fivefold. Per capita income growth is not the only indicator of welfare. Over the long run, there has been a dramatic increase in life expectation. In the year 1000, the average infant could expect to live about 24 years. A third would die in the first year of life, hunger and epidemic disease would ravage the survivors. There was an almost imperceptible rise up to 1820, mainly in Western Europe. Most of the improvement has occurred since then.

Now the average infant can expect to survive 66 years. The growth process was uneven in space as well as time. The rise in life expectation and income has been most rapid in Western Europe, North America, Australasia and Japan. By 1820, this group had forged ahead to an income level twice that in the rest of the world. By 1998, the gap was 7:1. Between the United States (the present world leader) and Africa (the poorest region) the gap is now 20:1. This gap is still widening. Divergence is dominant but not inexorable. In the past half century, resurgent Asian countries have demonstrated that an important degree of catch-up is feasible. Nevertheless world economic growth has slowed substantially since 1973, and the Asian advance has been offset by stagnation or retrogression elsewhere...

The purpose of this book is to quantify these long term changes in world income and population in a comprehensive way; identify the forces which explain the success of the rich countries; explore the obstacles which hindered advance in regions which lagged behind; scrutinize the interaction between the rich countries and the rest to assess the degree to which their backwardness may have been due to Western policy...

Explaining Economic Performance. Advances in population and income over the past millennium have been sustained by three interactive processes: a) Conquest or settlement of relatively empty areas which had fertile land, new biological resources, or a potential to accommodate transfers of population, crops and livestock; b) international trade and capitl movements; c) technological and institutional innovation.

a) Conquest and Settlement

One important instance of this process was Chinese settlement of the relatively empty and swampy lands south of the Yangtse, and introduction of new quick–ripening strains of rice from Vietnam suitable for multicropping. This process occurred between the eighth and thirteenth centuries, during which population growth accelerated, per capita income rose by a third, and the distribution of population and economic activity were transformed. In the eighth century only a quarter of the Chinese population lived south of the Yangtse; in the thirteenth, more than threequarters. The new technology involved higher labour inputs, so productivity rose less than per capita income.

An even more dramatic case was the European encounter with the Americas. The existence of this continent was unknown to Europeans before the 1492 voyage of Columbus. The discovery opened up an enormous area, for the most part thinly populated. Mexico and Peru were the most advanced and densely settled, but they were easily conquered and three quarters of their population was wiped out by diseases which the Europeans inadvertently introduced. The new continent offered crops unknown elsewhere — maize, potatoes, sweet potatoes, manioc, chilis, tomatoes, groundnuts, pineapples, cocoa and tobacco. These were introduced in Europe, Africa and Asia, and enhanced their production potential and capacity to sustain population growth. There was a reciprocal transfer to the Americas, which greatly augmented its potential. The new crops were wheat, rice, sugar cane, vines, salad greens, olives, bananas and coffee. The new animals for food were cattle, pigs, chickens, sheep and goats, as well as horses, oxen, asses and donkeys for transport.

The major initial attractions of the Americas were the rich silver resources of Mexico and Peru, and development of plantation agriculture with imports of slave labour from Africa. The neo–European economies of North America and the southern cone of Latin America developed later. The population of the Americas did not recover its 1500 level until the first half of the eighteenth century. The full potential of the Americas began to be realised in the nineteenth century with massive European immigration and the western movement of the production frontier made possible by railways.

The present variation in economic performance within the Americas — between the UnitedStates, Latin America and the Caribbean — is partly due to variations in resource endowment, but there are institutional and societal echoes from the past. In North America and Brazil the relatively small indigenous population was marginalised or exterminated, in former Spanish colonies the indigenous population remained as an underclass, and in all the areas where slavery was important their descendants have also remained an underprivileged group. Quite apart from this, there were important differences in the colonial period between Iberian institutions and those of North America.

These continued to have an impact on subsequent growth performance.

b) International Trade and Capital Movements

International trade was important in the economic ascension of Western Europe, and much less significant in the history of Asia or Africa.

Venice played a key role from 1000 to 1500 in opening up trade within Europe (to Flanders, France, Germany and the Balkans) and in the Mediterranean. It opened trade in Chinese products via the caravan routes to ports in the Black Sea. It traded in Indian and other Asian products via Syria and Alexandria. Trade was important in bringing high value spices and silks to Europe, but it also helped the transfer of technology from Asia, Egypt and Byzantium (silk and cotton textile production, glassblowing, cultivation of rice in Italy, cane sugar production and processing in the Venetian colonies of Crete and Cyprus). To a significant degree the maritime expansion of Venice depended on improved techniques of shipbuilding in its Arsenal, use of the compass and other improvements in navigation.

Institutional innovations — the development of banking, accountancy, foreign exchange and credit markets, creation of a solvent system of public finance, creation of a competent diplomatic service were all instrumental in establishing Venice as the lead economy of that epoch. Venice played an important part in fostering the intellectual development of Western Europe. It created manuscript libraries and pioneered in book publishing. Its glass industry was the first to make spectacles on a large scale. It played a leading role in the Renaissance by making Greek works known in the West. The University of Padua was a major centre of European learning, with Galileo as one of its distinguished professors.

Venetian contacts with Asia were eventually blocked by the fall of Byzantium, the rise of theOttoman Empire, the collapse of the crusader states in the Levant and the Mameluke regime in Egypt.

In the second half of the fifteenth century, a much more ambitious interaction between Europe and the rest of the world had started in Portugal.

Portugal played the main role in opening up European trade, navigation and settlement in the Atlantic islands, in developing trade routes around Africa, into the Indian Ocean, to China and Japan.

It became the major shipper of spices to Europe for the whole of the sixteenth century, usurping this role from

Venice. Its navigators discovered Brazil. Its diplomacy was astute enough to persuade Spain to endorse its territorial claim there, and to let it have a monopoly of trade with the Moluccan spice islands and Indonesia. Although Spain had a bigger empire, its only significant base outside the Americas was the Philippines. Its two most famous navigators were Columbus who was a Genoese with Portuguese training, and Magellan who was Portuguese. Portugal had major advantages in developing its overseas commerce and empire. There was a clear strategic benefit in being located on the South Atlantic coast of Europe near to the exit of the Mediterranean. Deep–sea fishermen provided an important part of the Portuguese food supply and developed an unrivalled knowledge of Atlantic winds, weather and tides. The value of these skills was greatly enhanced by crown sponsorship of Atlantic exploration, research on navigation, training of pilots, and documentation of maritime experience in the form of route maps with compass bearings (rutters) and cartography. Portuguese shipbuilders in Lisbon and Oporto adapted the design of their ships in the light of increasing knowledge of Atlantic sailing conditions. The biggest changes were in rigging. At first they concentrated on lateen sails, then added a mix of square sails and lateen for deeper penetration into the South Atlantic, with further changes for the much longer route round the Cape. Another element in Portuguese success was the ability to absorb "new Christians" — Jewish merchants and scholars who had played a significant role in Iberia during Muslim rule. They were driven out of Spain, but many took refuge and increased the size of the community in Portugal. They were required to undergo proforma conversion and were subject to a degree of persecution, but they provided important skills in developing Portuguese business interests in Africa, Brazil and Asia, in scientific development, as intermediaries in trade with the Muslim world and in attracting Genoese and Catalan capital to Portuguese business ventures.

Portugal was responsible for transferring cane sugar production and processing technology into the Atlantic islands of Madeira and São Tomé, and later to Brazil. It inaugurated the slave trade to provide a labour force for the industry in the New World. It carried about half of the slaves who were shipped to the Americas from Africa between 1500 and 1870. In the fifteenth century, sugar was a very rare and expensive commodity in Europe; by the end of the eighteenth century it was an item of popular consumption, having grown much more in volume than trade in any other tropical product.

At the time Portugal was pioneering these worldwide linkages, trade relations between different parts of northern Europe were intensified by the phenomenal development of Dutch maritime activity. In 1570, the carrying capacity of Dutch merchant shipping was about the same as the combined fleets of England, France and Germany. Per head of population it was 25 times as big as in these three northern countries.

Development of shipping and shipbuilding, the transformation of Dutch agriculture into horticulture, the creation of a large canal network, use of power derived from windmills and peat made the Netherlands the most dynamic European economy from 1400 to the middle of the seventeenth century. It pushed international specialisation much further than any other country. Shipping and commercial services provided a large part of its income. It imported cereals and live cattle, exported herring and dairy products. In 1700 only 40 per cent of the labour force were in agriculture.

Until 1580 the Netherlands was part of a bigger political entity. It included Flanders and Brabant — the most prosperous industrial area in Europe and a centre for banking, finance and international commerce which was a northern counterpart to Venice. The whole area was under Burgundian control until the late fifteenth century, then fell into the hands of the Habsburgs who were also rulers of Spain.

The Dutch revolted against their predatory empire because of its excessive fiscal demands, political and religious repression. They created a modern nation state, which protected property rights of merchants and entrepreneurs, promoted secular education and practised religious tolerance. Most of the financial and entrepreneurial elite and many of the most skilled artisans of Flanders and Brabant emigrated to the new republic. The Dutch blockaded the river Scheldt and the port of Antwerp for more than 200 years, and destroyed the Iberian monopoly of trade with Africa, Asia and the Americas. Dutch experience from 1580 to the end of the Napoleonic wars provides a dramatic demonstration of the way in which Western Europe interacted with the world economy in that epoch. The initial economic success of the Dutch Republic, and its maritime and commercial supremacy, depended to a substantial extent on success in war and beggar–your–neighbour commercial policy in competition with Portugal and Spain. By the eighteenth century it had lost this supremacy, because two new rivals, England and France, had greatly increased their maritime strength, and used the same techniques to push the Dutch out of the markets they sought to dominate. The volume of Dutch foreign trade dropped 20 per cent from 1720 to 1820. During this period, UK exports rose more than sevenfold in volume, and French by two and threequarters. From 1700 to 1820, Dutch per capita income fell by a sixth, British rose by half and French by a quarter. Britain had faster growth in per capita income from the 1680s to 1820 than any other European country. This was due to improvement of its banking, financial and fiscal institutions and agriculture on lines which the Dutch had pioneered, and to a surge in industrial productivity at the end of the period. It also derived great benefits from its rise to commercial hegemony by adroit use of a beggar–your–neighbour strategy.

Sixty years of armed conflict and the restrictive Navigation Acts pushed competitors out of the markets it sought to monopolise. It took over the leading role in shipping slaves from Africa to the Caribbean and created an overseas empire with a population of about 100 million by 1820. Other European powers were losers in the British struggle for supremacy. By the end of the Napoleonic wars, the Dutch had lost all their Asian territories except Indonesia. The French were reduced to a token colonial presence in Asia, and lost their major asset in the Caribbean. Shortly after the war, Brazil established its independence from Portugal. Spain lost its huge colonial empire in Latin America, retaining only Cuba, Puerto Rico and the Philippines. Britain took over what the French and Dutch had lost in Asia and Africa, extended its control over India, and established a privileged commercial presence in Latin America.

Other losers included the former rulers of India, whose power and income were usurped in substantial part by the servants of the British East India Company. Under their rule, from 1757 to 1857, Indian per capita income fell, but British gains were substantial.

Between 1820 and 1913, British per capita income grew faster than at any time in the past — three times as fast as in 1700–1820. The basic reason for improved performance was the acceleration of technical progress, accompanied by rapid growth of the physical capital stock and improvement in the education and skills of the labour force, but changes in commercial policy also made a substantial contribution. In 1846 protective duties on agricultural imports were removed and in 1849 the Navigation Acts were terminated. By 1860, all trade and tariff restrictions had been removed unilaterally. In 1860 there were reciprocal treaties for freer trade with France and other European countries. These had most–favoured nation clauses which meant that bilateral liberalisation applied equally to all countries.Free trade was imposed in India and other British colonies, and the same was true in Britain's informal empire. China, Persia, Thailand and the Ottoman Empire were not colonies, but were obliged to maintain low tariffs by treaties which reduced their sovereignty in commercial matters, and granted extraterritorial rights to foreigners. This regime of free trade imperialism favoured British exports, but was less damaging to the interests of the colonies than in the eighteenth century, when Jamaica could only trade with Britain and its colonies, Guadeloupe only with France. The British policy of free trade and its willingness to import a large part of its food had positive effects on the world economy. They reinforced and diffused the impact of technical progress. The favourable impact was biggest in North America, the southern cone of Latin America and Australasia which had rich natural resources and received a substantial inflow of capital, but there was also some positive effect in India which was the biggest and poorest part of the Empire. Innovations in communications played a major part in linking national capital markets and facilitating international capital movements. The United Kingdom already had an important role in international finance, thanks to the soundness of its public credit and monetary system, the size of its capital market and public debt, and the maintenance of a gold standard since 1821 to stabilise its exchange rate. The existence of the empire had created a system of property rights which appeared to be as securely protected as those available to investors in British securities. It was a wealthy country operating close to the frontiers of technology, so its rentiers were attracted by foreign investment opportunities even when the extra margin of profit was small.

From the 1870s onward there was a massive outflow of British capital for overseas investment. The UK directed about half of its savings abroad. French, German and Dutch investment was also substantial. By 1913, British foreign assets were equivalent to one and a half times its GDP, income from them meant that national income was more than 9 per cent greater than its domestic product. Table 2–26a shows the origin and location of this foreign capital as it stood in 1914. Movement of capital made a significant contribution to growth in Australia, Canada, New Zealand, Argentina, Southern Brazil, Uruguay, Russia and South Africa, but its per capita impact was small in Asia. Most of it was in the form of bonds and a good deal was in railways. From 1870 to 1913, world capita GDP rose 1.3 per cent a year compared with 0.5 per cent in 1820–70 and 0.07 per cent in 1700–1820. The acceleration was due to more rapid technological progress, and to the diffusionist forces unleashed by the liberal economic order of which the United Kingdom was the main architect. It was not a process of global equalisation, but there were significant income gains in all parts of the world. Australia and the United States reached higher levels than the United Kingdom by 1913. Growth was faster than in the United Kingdom in most of Western and Eastern Europe, in Ireland, in all the Western Offshoots, in Latin America and

Japan. In India, other Asia (except China) and Africa, the advances were much more modest, but per capita income rose more than a quarter between 1870 to 1913. Trade grew faster than income on a world basis and in virtually all countries from 1870 to 1913

In all of these dimensions, the situation was an enormous improvement on the eighteenth century, when shipments of slaves were bigger than the movement of migrants, when capital flows and transfer of technology were of limited significance, and when commercial policy was conducted on a beggar– your–neighbour basis. Keynes (1919, pp. 9–10) provides an illuminating patrician perspective on the lifestyle and investment opportunities available to people like himself in Britain at the end of the liberal era:

"The inhabitant of London could order by telephone, sipping his morning tea in bed, the various products of the whole earth, in such quantity as he might see fit, and reasonably expect their early delivery on his doorstep; he could at the same moment and by the same means adventure his wealth in the natural resources and new enterprise of any quarter of the world. He could secure forthwith, if he wished it, cheap and comfortable means of transport to any country or climate without passport or other formality, could despatch his servant to the neighbouring office of a bank for such supply of the precious metals as might seem convenient, and then proceed abroad to foreign quarters, without knowledge of their religion, language, or customs, bearing coined wealth upon his person, and would consider himself greatly aggrieved and much surprised at the least interference — He regarded this state of affairs as normal, certain, and permanent."

Wars, Depression and Exit from Empire, 1913–50 This was a complex and dismal period, marked deeply by the shock of two world wars and an intervening depression. The liberal economic order was shattered. World trade was much smaller in relation to world income in 1950 than it had been in 1913. International migration was a fraction of what it had been in the nineteenth century. Most of Western Europe's foreign assets were sold, seized or destroyed. Overseas empires disappeared or were in an advanced state of disintegration. In spite of these disastrous shocks, and drastic reorientation of economic policy and policy instruments, their impact on world economic growth was smaller than might have been expected because the pace of technological advance was substantially faster in the twentieth century than in the nineteenth.

Development of road vehicles sustained the earlier transport revolution. The number of passenger cars in Western Europe rose from about 300 000 in 1913 to nearly 6 million in 1950, and from 1.1 to 40 million in the United States (see Maddison, 1995a, p. 72). There was a parallel transformation of road freight transport, and tractors had a significant impact in replacing horses in agriculture. Aviation had its main impact before 1950 on the technique of warfare, but its economic role in shrinking the significance of distance was already clear.

Development of electricity to produce heat, light and power also had massive ramifications: "electricity freed the machine and tool from the bondage of place; it made power ubiquitous and placed it within the reach of everyone" (Landes, 1966, p. 509). It made it possible to create new kinds of factories to assemble and mass produce automobiles and a huge range of new household products — sewing machines, refrigerators, washing machines, vacuum cleaners, radios and cameras. It contributed to a vastly popular new brand of popular cinematic entertainment. There were important advances in chemistry, which made it possible to create synthetic materials, fertilisers, pharmaceuticals which had important implications for economic potential and medicine. The leading role in developing these twentieth century technologies was played by the United States, which had become the world leader in terms of productivity and per capita income. The driving forces of innovation had changed from the nineteenth century, with a reduced role for the individual inventor, and greater emphasis on applied scientific research of a type which the United States pioneered. It institutionalised innovation in a way the United Kingdom had never done. In 1913, there were about 370 research units in US manufacturing employing 3 500 people. By 1946 there were 2 300 units employing 118 000. In 1946 there were four scientific workers in US manufacturing per 1 000 wage earners, five times the ratio in the United Kingdom. US government–sponsored research played a much more important role in agriculture and mining than in the United Kingdom, and the link between business firms and universities was closer (see Mowery and Rosenberg, 1989).

The United States developed new forms of professional business management, where large enterprises played a strategic role in standardising and enlarging markets. Multi–unit firms coordinated advertising, packaging, transport, sales and marketing. They allocated large amounts of capital, spread risks and increased productivity over a large range of new industries.

It is not easy to provide an aggregative estimate of the pace of technical change or its acceleration, but a rough proxy measure is the pace of advance in total factor productivity (the response of output to combined inputs of labour and capital) in the lead country with the highest productivity level. By 1913, it was the United States, not Britain, which operated closest to the technological frontier. Between 1913 and 1950, US total factor productivity grew by 1.6 per cent a year, more than four times as fast as it or the United Kingdom had achieved from 1870 to 1913. This was the first stage of a technological boom which lasted for 60 years. An acceleration of total factor productivity growth also occurred in the United Kingdom in 1913–50, though to a lesser degree than in the United States (see Maddison 1995a, pp. 40–50, and 252–5). There was also an associated acceleration of growth of labour productivity in most West European countries (see Appendix E, Table E–8). The importance of this acceleration in growth potential was masked by the interwar behaviour of the United States, and the nature of its economic policy. In the 1930s, it had transmitted a strong deflationary impulse to the world economy by its deep depression which was reinforced by raising its tariffs and withdrawal from foreign investment. In Europe its potential was muted by two world wars which involved diversion of massive resources to mutual destruction.

In the first world war, threequarters of a million British troops were killed in combat, and 7.8 million tons of shipping were lost (mainly in submarine attacks). But these losses were proportionately much smaller than those of France, Germany and Russia. The nominal value of its foreign assets was more or less the same at the end of the war as in 1914, whereas German assets were confiscated as reparations, and two thirds of French were lost through inflation and Russian default. Britain added to its overseas empire by acquiring Germany's former colonies in Tanganyika and Namibia, and took over former Turkish possessions in the Middle East (Iraq, Jordan and Palestine), but a large part of Ireland became an independent republic.

In the 1920s British growth was hampered by highly deflationary policies to drive down wages and maintain an overvalued currency at its prewar parity. Their objective was to restore London's prewar role as an international financial centre and to serve the interests of rentiers who held bonds denominated in sterling. As a consequence, there were high levels of unemployment and loss of competitiveness in export markets. Britain had the worst performance in Western Europe in the 1920s, in terms of GDP growth and exports.

The depression of the 1930s led to devaluation of sterling, a large cut in interest rates, an abandonment of free trade, and creation of a network of imperial preferences. These policies cushioned the impact of the world depression on domestic economy. Housing investment had been depressed by high interest rates in the 1920s, and responded very favourably to their decline. There was no British counterpart to the collapse of the banking system which took place in the United States, Germany and Austria. Exports to the empire were bolstered by devaluation and imperial tariff preferences. As a result the impact of the world depression was milder in the United Kingdom than in all West European countries, except Denmark.

Britain came much closer to defeat in the second world war than in the first because Germany captured the whole of the West European continent in its rapid blitzkrieg. The eventual victory was due to very intensive domestic resource mobilisation, sale of foreign assets, financial, material and military support from the United States, Canada, India and Australasia, and Russian resistance to Germany on the Eastern front.

The war changed the economics of empire. The Japanese quickly conquered British colonies in East Asia which could not be adequately defended. The strength of the nationalist movement made it politically necessary to finance military expenditure in India by borrowing rather than local taxation.

As a result India was able to liquidate $1.2 billion of prewar debt and acquired sterling balances worth more than $5 billion. The costs of maintaining the empire now greatly outweighed the benefits, and the acceleration of technical progress had reinforced the attractions of domestic investment.

The British withdrawal from India occurred in 1947, from Sri Lanka and Burma in 1948. The withdrawal from the

African colonies followed a few years after the United States demanded the withdrawal of British forces from Egypt in 1956. The British imperial order was finished, as were those of Belgium, France, the Netherlands and Japan. In the West, the United States had emerged as the hegemonial power competing with the Soviet bloc for leverage in the newly independent countries of Africa and Asia. The foreign economic and commercial policy of the United States was very different from its prewar stance. It made major efforts to diffuse technology, to promote the outflow of capital and liberalisation of world trade. This new orientation was already manifest in 1948 in Marshall Plan aid for European reconstruction.

The impact of British expansion in the Americas, Africa and Asia

As Europe's major offshore island, Britain always had substantial overseas involvements. Until the eleventh century, Britain was a target for conquest and barbarian invasion. Between the twelfth to the fifteenth centuries, under the Norman and Angevin dynasties, it was heavily engaged in attempts to acquire territory in France.

Thereafter Britain was involved in many wars in Europe, mainly with Spain, France and the Netherlands, but the objectives were commercial or diplomatic. By the middle of the sixteenth century, the idea of European conquest had been abandoned. Although trade was developed in the Baltic and Mediterranean overseas ambitions were concentrated on the Americas and Asia. Until the nineteenth century the only significant interest in Africa was the slave trade.

In the sixteenth century, the main activities outside Europe were piracy and reconnoitring voyages to explore the potential for developing a colonial empire. The boldest stroke was royal backing for the 1577–80 voyage of Drake, who took five ships and 116 men, rounded the Straits of Magellan, seized and plundered Spanish treasure ships off the coast of Chile and Peru, made useful contacts in the spice islands of the Moluccas, Java, the Cape of Good Hope and Guinea on his way back.

Piracy and Britain's support of the Dutch Republic provoked war with Spain from 1585 which lasted two decades. By this time, its maritime strength and skill were adequate to defeat the Spanish Armada. This was an invasion force of 130 ships from Cadiz which intended to rendezvous with a fleet of invasion barges in the Spanish Netherlands. The British victory at Gravelines prevented the rendezvous and forced the Spanish fleet to return home around the northwest of Scotland. Spain lost more than half of its fleet, and it was clear that Britain had acquired the naval power to support major ventures in the Americas and Asia.

As overseas ventures were varied in character and became bigger in scope than those of any other European power, our survey is necessarily selective and is presented below under four headings:

a) development of sugar colonies in the Caribbean and associated participation in the slave trade from Africa from the 1620s onwards;

b) settlement of 13 colonies in North America between 1607 and 1713 which became the United States in 1776;

c) creation of an East Indian Trading Company in 1600 and its conquest of an Indian Empire after 1757;

d) forcible opening of trade with China and establishment of the Treaty Port regime of free trade imperialism.

a) The Caribbean and the Slave Trade

The Caribbean islands were the first Spanish possessions in the Americas, but the native Arawaks in Hispaniola (Haiti and Dominican Republic) were quickly wiped out by disease and the Caribs in the Antilles were greatly depleted. Spanish interest switched to Peru and Mexico once large scale silver production started there in the middle of the sixteenth century. The British occupied the uninhabited island of Barbados in 1627 establishing tobacco plantations with a labour force of indentured white settlers. Dutch shippers in the Brazilian sugar trade promoted the idea of developing Caribbean sugar production with slave labour. Dutch entrepreneurs established sugar plantations in Barbados when they were expelled from Brazil. As the island was well watered, and the winds were favourable for a quick passage to Europe, it became Britain's biggest sugar colony until Jamaica was captured from Spain in 1655. With similar help from the Dutch, the French developed sugar production in Martinique and Guadeloupe and later took over a much bigger area in Saint Domingue (Haiti). The Dutch were pushed out of the British and French colonies and created a smaller sugar economy in Surinam. Britain took some French islands (St. Vincent,

Grenada, Dominica and Tobago) in 1763, and Trinidad from Spain in 1727. British entry to the slave trade was pioneered by Hawkins in 1562. Participation reached its peak in the seventeenth and eighteenth centuries when Britain became the main slave shipper, bringing a total of 2.5 million Africans to the Americas (see Table 2–5). The traffic was heaviest to the Caribbean. The British staked out Sierra Leone and the upper Guinea coast in the seventeenth century as their source of supply, the French took slaves mainly from the Senegal–Gambia region and the Dutch from the Gold Coast. The Portuguese operated the Africa–Brazil trade further south in Angola. The Royal Africa Company had a monopoly on British slave trading from 1672 to 1698, but in the eighteenth century "individual entrepreneurs who organised one or several voyages had become the norm in the trade" (see Klein, 1999, p. 80). Apart from European traders, there was financial backing from merchants in New England, Virginia, the West Indies and Brazil. Slavers generally financed their purchases with trade goods (East Indian textiles, alcohol, tobacco, bar iron, weapons, jewellery, or cowrie shells from the Maldives — for use in Africa as currency). "In the overwhelming majority of cases it was the Africans who controlled the slaves until their moment of sale to the captain — African slave traders came down to the coast or the riverbanks in a relatively steady and predictable stream to well–known trading places — European traders tended to spend months on the coast or travelling upriver gathering their slaves a few at a time" (Klein, 1999, pp. 90–1).

Within Africa, slaves were acquired as captives in local wars, as tribute from dependent tribes, or after condemnation as criminals, but there was also large scale slave raiding and kidnapping of individuals within Africa. Klein (1999, p. 129) estimated that of 18 million African slaves exported from 1500 to 1900, "11 million of them were shipped into the Atlantic economy. The other slaves were shipped into the Indian Ocean or across the Sahara to slave markets in the East."

The normal cargo per ship ranged between 400–500 slaves. Klein (1999, p. 139) estimates 12 per cent average mortality on the passage to America over the period 1590–1867 which he compares with 10 per cent in convict ships on the longer voyage to Australia in 1787–1800.[unquote][59]

The devastation caused by colonial domination and colonial loot has to be undone and a new era of socio-economic development has to be realised.

Making common cause to gain multiplier effects with specific developmental projects

"Since there are almost 7 billion people alive today, it follows that they are making seven times as much history as the 1 billion alive in 1811. The chart below shows a population-weighted history of the past two millennia. By this reckoning, over 28% of all the history made since the birth of Christ was made in the 20th century. Measured in years lived, the present century, which is only ten years old, is already "longer" than the whole of the 17th century. This century has made an even bigger contribution to economic history. Over 23% of all the goods and services made since 1AD were produced from 2001 to 2010, according to an updated version of Angus Maddison's figures."

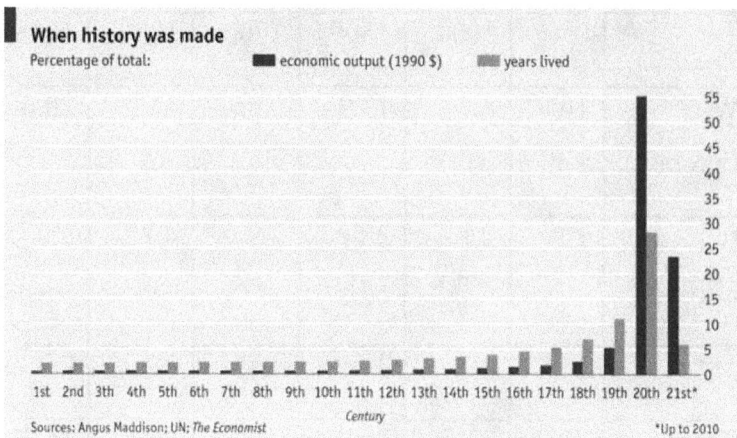

1st 2nd 3th 4th 5th 6th 7th 8th 9th 10th 11th 12th 13th 14th 15th 16th 17th 18th 19th 20th 21st*

Century

Sources: Angus Maddison; UN; *The Economist*   *Up to 2010

In the first decade of the 21st century, the population of the world produced more economic output than in the first 19 centuries of the common era combined.[60]

How to create a multiplier effect to accelerate the pace of development of the Indian Ocean Community?Asia accounted for 75.1% of world GDP at the turn of the Common Era. It declined to 36.0% in 1870 and to 29.5 in 1998. Africa's share for the turn of the Common Era, 1870 and 1998 were: 6.8%, 3.6% and 3.1%. Most of the Indian Ocean Countries are in these Asia and Africa regions and all of them were impoverished, registerin steep declines in their share of the world GDP.

Shares of World GDP, select countries, regional totals

	0	1000	1500	1700	1870	1998
W. Europe	10.8	8.7	17.9	22.5	33.6	20.6
E. Europe	1.9	2.2	2.5	2.9	4.1	2.0
Japan	1.2	2.7	3.1	4.1	2.3	7.7
China	28.2	22.7	25.0	22.3	8.9	11.5
India	32.9	28.9	24.5	24.4	7.6	5.0
Other Asia	16.1	16.0	12.7	10.9	5.4	13.0
Total Asia (excldg. Japan)	75.1	67.6	62.1	57.6	21.9	29.5
Africa	6.8	11.8	7.4	6.6	2.7	3.1
WORLD	100	100	100	100	100	100
	0	1000	1500	1700	1870	1998

This was counterbalanced by the increase in the wealth of Western offshoots from a share of 0.5 at the turn of the Common Era to 30.6% in 1950 and 25.1% in 1998

The principal objective of establishing Indian Ocean Community is to restore Asia and Africa to the share the continents had at the turn of the common era (0 CE): to 83.1% of World GDP (from the 19998 level of 40.3%).

Source: Table B-20, Maddison; Contours of the World Economy 1-2030 CE by Angus Maddison (2007)[61]

Table 2: Basic Economic Indicators by Region and Subregion

	Share of World Population (%) 2010	Share of World GDP (%, PPP) 2011	Real GDP Growth (%)[1]		Per Capita GDP (PPP)	
			Average 2000–2007	Average 2008-2011	$ 2011	Average Growth (%) 2000–2007
Asia	56.2	36.6	6.2	5.8	7,376	7.0
East Asia	22.5	23.5	6.3	5.9	11,896	7.7
Central Asia	1.2	0.7	10.3	5.9	6,396	9.8
Southeast Asia	8.7	4.2	5.5	4.5	5,476	6.0
South Asia	23.3	6.9	6.8	7.0	3,325	7.4
The Pacific and Oceania	0.5	1.3	3.4	2.0	29,623	3.5
European Union	7.2	20.1	2.6	0.0	31,607	3.6
North America	6.6	23.0	2.6	0.4	39,450	3.1
World[2]	100.0	100.0	4.2	2.8	10,821	4.7

GDP = gross domestic product, PPP = purchasing power parity.
Notes: The list of countries in each subregion is shown in Table 3. European Union (EU) refers to the aggregate of the 27 EU members. North America includes Canada, Mexico, and the United States.
[1]Weighted by nominal GDP in PPP.
[2]Per capita GDP as of end-2010.
Source: ADB calculations using data from *Asian Development Outlook 2012*, Asian Development Bank; *World Economic Outlook Database April 2012*, International Monetary Fund; and *World Development Indicators*, World Bank.

Table 5: Trade-to-GDP Ratio by Region and Subregion (%)

	1990	2000	2010	2011
Asia	**30.1**	**40.4**	**54.1**	**57.3**
East Asia	26.7	34.1	51.1	52.8
People's Republic of China	29.9	39.6	50.2	49.9
Southeast Asia	89.4	130.8	107.2	116.1
ASEAN-4	62.9	103.7	78.1	86.0
BCLMV	75.3	84.4	110.1	130.8
Singapore	293.1	289.3	292.3	299.4
Central Asia	–	62.8	52.4	59.7
South Asia	16.0	23.0	36.7	44.0
India	12.9	19.5	35.9	44.2
The Pacific and Oceania	28.3	37.3	36.3	37.8
European Union	–	**57.6**	**62.5**	**67.2**
North America	**18.4**	**25.6**	**27.4**	**29.9**
World	**31.1**	**40.2**	**48.0**	**51.9**

ASEAN-4 = Indonesia, Malaysia, the Philippines, and Thailand; BCLMV = Brunei Darussalam, Cambodia, the Lao People's Democratic Republic, Myanmar, and Viet Nam; GDP = gross domestic product; North America = Canada, Mexico, and the United States; – = unavailable.
Notes: Figures refer to the ratio of total trade to gross domestic product (GDP) for the specified years. Values were derived by dividing total trade (exports plus imports) by nominal GDP (both in $).
Source: ADB calculations using data from *Direction of Trade Statistics* and *World Economic Outlook Database April 2012*, International Monetary Fund; and CEIC for Taipei,China.

Table 1: Regional GDP Growth[1] (y-o-y, %)

	2009	2010	2011	ADB Forecast 2012	ADB Forecast 2013
Developing Asia	6.0	9.1	7.2	6.6	7.1
Central Asia[2]	3.2	6.6	6.2	5.8	6.2
East Asia[3]	6.8	9.8	8.0	7.1	7.5
PRC	9.2	10.4	9.2	8.2	8.5
South Asia[4]	7.5	7.7	6.2	6.2	6.9
India	8.4	8.4	6.5	6.5	7.3
Southeast Asia[5]	1.4	7.9	4.6	5.2	5.6
The Pacific[6]	4.3	5.5	7.0	6.0	4.2
Major Industrialized economies					
United States	-3.5	3.0	1.7	1.9	2.2
eurozone	-4.4	2.0	1.5	-0.7	0.8
Japan	-5.5	4.4	-0.7	2.2	1.5

PRC = People's Republic of China, GDP = gross domestic product, eurozone = Austria,
Belgium, Cyprus, Estonia, Finland, France, Germany, Greece, Ireland, Italy, Luxembourg, Malta,
the Netherlands, Portugal, Slovakia, Slovenia, and Spain.
[1] Aggregates are weighted according to gross national income levels (Atlas method, current $)
from World Development Indicators, World Bank.
[2] Includes Armenia, Azerbaijan, Georgia, Kazakhstan, the Kyrgyz Republic, Tajikistan,
Turkmenistan, and Uzbekistan.
[3] Includes the People's Republic of China; Hong Kong, China; the Republic of Korea; Mongolia;
and Taipei,China.
[4] Includes Afghanistan, Bangladesh, Bhutan, India, Republic of the Maldives, Nepal, Pakistan,
and Sri Lanka. Data for Bangladesh, India, and Pakistan are recorded on a fiscal-year basis.
For India, the fiscal year spans the current year's April through the next year's March. For
Bangladesh and Pakistan, the fiscal year spans the previous year's July through the current
year's June.
[5] Includes Brunei Darussalam, Cambodia, Indonesia, the Lao People's Democratic Republic,
Malaysia, the Philippines, Singapore, Thailand, and Viet Nam. Excludes Myanmar as weights
unavailable.
[6] Includes the Cook Islands, Fiji, Kiribati, the Marshall Islands, the Federated States of Micronesia,
Nauru, Palau, Papua New Guinea, Samoa, Solomon Islands, Timor-Leste, Tonga, Tuvalu,
and Vanuatu.

Basic economic indicators of 'Developing Asia' such as population data, GDP, Trade-to-GDP ratio, are provided in a July 2012 publication (Titled as Tables 2 and 5).There are indications of increasing trade within the region itself as Asia's share of world exports rose from 23.4% in 1990 to 34.3% in 2011. By 2050, the region could exceed 50% of global trade. The following table (also taken from the same publication)[62] shows GDP growth (year-on-year) in 'Developing Asia' (which includes many countries of the Indian Ocean Community compared with the GDP growth in major industrialized economies. Though the growth rates between 2009 and 2012 range between 1.4 to 9.2% in most Indian Ocean Community nations, the rates are a slow process of catch-up to attain the situation which existed before the colonial era.

The pace of growth has to be quickened and the multiplier effect can be provided by the formation of Indian Ocean Community.

A relativist theory for wealth of nations

A theory of wealth of nations is a return to Adam Smith's view of Economics and an economic theory for Artha (wealth) founded on the global ethic – Dharma-Dhamma.

The following axioms or basic principles help identify the foundations of Dharma-Dhamma economics and provide a framework for a relativist theory of wealth of nations.[63]

Axiom 1

Man is an inquirer. Four puruṣārthas or goals of life are: Dharma, Artha, Kāma, Mokṣa i.e., respectively:

- eternal law, righteousness, ethikos,

- livelihood, wealth,

- sensual pleasure

- liberation, freedom from samsāra

Thus, man, in this inquiry or quest, deploys material resources, work, governed by the eternal law.

Dharma is not just law, or harmony, it is pure Reality. In the Brihadarnyaka Upanishad:

Verily, that which is Dharma is truth, Therefore they say of a man who speaks truth, "He speaks the Dharma," or of a man who speaks the Dharma, "He speaks the Truth.", Verily, both these things are the same.
—(*Brh. Upanishad*, 1.4.14)

Creation Hymn of the Rig Veda, Nasadiya Sukta, says:

Who really knows?
Who will here proclaim it?
Whence was it produced? Whence is this creation?
The gods came afterwards, with the creation of this universe.
Who then knows whence it has arisen?

Whence this creation has arisen - perhaps it has

formed itself, or perhaps it did not

The one who looks down on it, in the highest heaven,

Only he knows - or perhaps he does not know.

ātman is eternal, is ultimately indistinct from Brahman, the supreme *ātman, paramātman*. The goal of life is to realize this. This realization is liberation, mokṣa.

Axiom 2

Protection of wealth. This includes absence of covetousness and ethical practices in work.

Axiom 3

Acquisition of artha, wealth is a virtue so long as it is acquired honestly with due regard to social responsibility that accompanies the acquisition. Wealth is a means of fulfilling one's responsibility, svadharma, in the world. This is in sharp contract to the Christian view that true ownership belongs only to God as expressed by Augustine in the fifth century: "Since every earthly possession can be rightly retained only on the ground either of divine right, according to which all things belong to the Righteous [i.e., God], or of human right, which is in the jurisdiction of the kings of the earth, you are mistaken in calling those things yours which you do not possess...". (Augustine, *Patrologiae Latinae*, ed. J.P. Migne (Paris, 1844-1864), Letter 133, 12, vol. 33; cited in Richard Schlatter, *Private Property* (London: Allen and Unwin, 1951), p. 37.) This Christian view led to theories of socialism/communism and denial of individual ownership rights, restricting them only to *licenses of use*.

Axiom 4

Every *ātman* is entitled to take pleasure in the world, without denying oneself the experiences of this world. Karma, which literally means 'work' or 'act', is a universal principle of cause and effect, beneficial effects are derived from beneficial actions. Thus work is exertion of control over the material in order to realize one's divine potential, in every *ātman*. Every *ātman* is rooted in the material world, an integral part of material existence. Every *ātman* is a portion of the *paramātman,* the supreme divinity. Every *ātman* is thus engaged in creative acts, creative development of the world of experiences. This axiom naturally leads to a clear perception of the institution of private property.

Axiom 5 Care for the needy. The word dharma or a synonym *dāna* itself has this obligation of active responsibility participating in acts of charity, caring for those in need. This commandment is exemplified in śreṇi dharma, the social responsibility of the guilds. Thus instead of imposing a commandment on enforced distribution of wealth, a level of moral and religious rectitude is expected of members of the guild to support the social causes such as maintenance of local irrigation tanks and drinking water wells and religious responsibilities exemplified by the building, maintenance of temples and supportive donations for temple festivities. The śreṇi dharma is thus a reaffirmation of personal responsibility, rather than a legally enforced principle or a contractual obligation. This axiom is comparable to the Judaic perspective of property as "an expression of man's sovereignty, his capacity to rule over the material world, so that he may benefit from it, care for it, and perfect it through creative acts."[64]

Axiom 6 In treatises of statecraft, measures are postulated to ensure that oppression of governance is kept in check.

Economics of happiness

More wants than resources creates scarcity. Scarcity is dealt with by a discipline called Economics.

MIT Dictionary of Modern Economics, befines economics as, "the study of the way in which mankind organizes itself to tackle the basic problem of scarcity. All societies have more wants than resources (the factors of production), so that a system must be devised to allocate these resources between competing ends."

The economic problem, therefore, begins with 'wants'. The problem is the craving for things, NOT the enjoyment of things. The problem is NOT with wealth, but with the ATTACHMENT to wealth.

An economist thinks that one who consumes more is better off than one who consumes less and thus measures 'standard of living' by the amount of one's annual consumption.

Consumption is but a means to one's well-being. The goal of economics should, therefore be, maximum well-being with minimum consumption. This will liberate a person with more discretionary time for the person's creative talents finding expression and realisation of one's fullest potential. This is the message of EF Shumacher in 'Small is Beautiful.'

The Declaration of Independenceb IN CONGRESS, July 4, 1776.
The unanimous Declaration of the thirteen united States of America,

When in the Course of human events, it becomes necessary for one people to dissolve the political bands which have connected them with another, and to assume among the powers of the earth, the separate and equal station to which the Laws of Nature and of Nature's God entitle them, a decent respect to the opinions of mankind requires that they should declare the causes which impel them to the separation.

We hold these truths to be self-evident, that all men are created equal, that they are endowed by their Creator with certain unalienable Rights, that among these are Life, Liberty and the pursuit of Happiness.--That to secure these rights, Governments are instituted among Men, deriving their just powers from the consent of the governed,---That whenever any Form of Government becomes destructive of these ends, it is the Right of the People to alter or to abolish it, and to institute new Government, laying its foundation on such principles and organizing its powers in such form, as to them shall seem most likely to effect their Safety and Happiness.

"In short, I am convinced, both by faith and experience, that to maintain one's self on this earth is not a hardship but a pastime, if we will live simply and wisely; It is not necessary that a man should earn his living by the sweat of his brow, unless he sweats easier than I do."[65]

In East Asia, the character for *Dharma* is 法, pronounced fǎ in Mandarin Chinese, hō in Japanese and beop in Korean. The Tibetan complete English translation of this term is chos (Tibetan: ཆོས་, Lhasa dialect IPA: [[tɕʰɵʔ]]). In Uyghur, Mongolian, and some other Central Asian languages, it is nom, which derives from the Ancient Greek word νόμος, *nómos*, meaning "law". Samskṛtam root for dharma (Pali dhamma) is: dhṛ 'to uphold, to support' semantically expanded as that which holds together fabric of reality, natural phenomena and personality of human beings in dynamic interdependence and harmony.

Six attributes of Buddha dhamma

1. Svākkhāto (Sanskrit: Svākhyāta "well proclaimed").
   Universal Law of Nature based on a causal analysis
   of natural phenomena. The course of study is
   'excellent in the beginning (sīla – Sanskrit śīla –
   moral principles), excellent in the middle
   (samādhi – concentration) and excellent in the end'
   (paññā - Sanskrit prajñā . . . Wisdom).

2. Sandiṭṭhiko (Sanskrit: Sāṃdṛṣṭika "able to be examined").

3. Akāliko (Sanskrit: Akālika "timeless, immediate").

4. Ehipassiko (Sanskrit: Ehipaśyika "which you can come and see" — from the phrase ehi, paśya "come, see!")..

5. Opanayiko (Sanskrit: Avapraṇayika "leading one close to").In the "Vishuddhimagga" "the path of purification", this is also referred to as "Upanayanam."

6. Paccattaṃ veditabbo viññūhi (Sanskrit: Pratyātmaṃ veditavyo vijñaiḥ "To be personally known by the wise").

This is an echo from the statement of Brihadaranyaka Upanishad:

sa naiva vyabhavat |
tac chreyo rūpam atyasṛjata dharmam |
tad etat kṣatrasya kṣatraṃ yad dharmaḥ |
tasmād dharmāt paraṃ nāsti |
atho abalīyān balīyāṃsam āśaṃsate dharmeṇa |
yathā rājñaivam |
yo vai sa dharmaḥ satyaṃ vai tat |

tasmāt satyaṃ vadantam āhur dharmaṃ vadatīti |

dharmaṃ vā vadantaṃ satyaṃ vadatīti |

etad dhy evaitad ubhayaṃ bhavati || BrhUp_1,4.14 ||

" Verily, that which is Dharma is truth.

Therefore they say of a man who speaks truth, 'He speaks the Dharma,'

Or of a man who speaks the Dharma, 'He speaks the Truth.'

Verily, both these things are the same."

(Brh. Upanishad, 1.4.14)

Pravṛtti-Nivṛtti: Social action, Personal knowledge

In Patanjali Yoga Sūtra 3.13 three aspects of change are identified:

transformation of a thing (dharmi) into a property (dharma),

transformation of a property into a mark (lakṣaṇa), and

the transformation of a mark into a condition (avasthā).

This is then the basis of the "unreasonable effectiveness" of mathematics in the description of the world.

Change applies both to physical substance (bhūta) and to the senses (indriya),i.e.,to sensations.

Pravṛtti relates to social action (trivarga: dharma, artha ka_ma == righteousness, prosperity. desire) Nivṛtti i relates to inward contemplation.

Addressing his father, Suka said: The declaration of the Vedas are twofold. They once lay down the command, "Do all acts." They also indicate the reverse saying, "Give up acts." Where do persons go by the aid of Knowledge and where by the aid of Acts? Indeed, these declarations about knowledge and acts are dissimilar and even contradictory. I desire to hear this. Do tell me this.

Vyāsa said: I shall expound to thee the two paths, viz., the destructible and the indestructible, depending respectively upon acts and knowledge. Listen with concentrated attention, O child, to me, as I tell thee the place that is reached by one with the aid of knowledge, and that other place which is reached with the aid of acts. The difference between these two places, is as great as the limitless sky. These are the two paths upon which the Vedas are established; the duties indicated by Pravṛtti, and those based on Nivṛtti.[66]

Gita propounds: "In this world there is a two fold path; the path of knowledge of the Sankhyas and the path of action of the Yogis." --"The Vedic dharma (religion) is verily two-fold, characterised by Pravṛtti (social action) and Nivṛtti (inward contemplation), designed to promote order in the world; this twofold dharma has in view the true social welfare and spiritual emancipation of all beings."[67]

The history of dharma and dhamma as regulatory principles of life and maintenance of order in the cosmos is exemplified by the following expositions, many of which are echoed in the ancient texts of Bauddham:

Kanada of Vaiśesṣika declares:

Athā to dharma vyā khyā syā mah Yatobhyudaya nihśreyasa siddhih sa dharmah (Vaiśesika Sutra 1.11.2)

Dharma is that which exalts and bestows the Supreme Good or Absolute Bliss (cessation of pain). "That which leads to the attainment of Abhyudaya (prosperity in this world) and Nihśreyasa (total cessation of pain and attainment of eternal bliss hereafter) is Dharma".

Note: *Kauśītakī Brāhmaṇa Upaniṣad* uses the term nihśreyas in the context of ātman: II-13. Now, with reference to the Self II-14. Now, next, the assumption of superior excellence. Ni*h*sreyasâdâna (the accepting of the pre-eminence of prâ*n*a (breath or life) by the other divinities). cf. Âṣvalâyana G*ṛ*ihya-sûtras I, 13, 7.

Rāṣṭram is the ātman. Country is the body. State is the protective robe.

A person with faith in dharma-dhamma realizes the fact that every living being and phenomenon on the globe is a divine manifestation. No dogma or doctrine governs the dharma-dhamma way of life. The only emphasis is on responsibility, duty: protection of dharma-dhamma since dharma-dhamma protects us. The accent is on collective responsibility, not on individual, atomised rights.

Bauddham exhorts: Buddham, dhamma, sangham śaraṇam gacchāmi.

Mahā nārayaṇopaniṣad (Section 79.7) declares thus:

dharmo viśvasya jagatah pratiṣṭhā

111

loke dharmiṣṭha prajā upasarpanti

dharmeṇa pāpamapanudati

dharme sarvam pratiṣṭhitam

tasmāddharmam paramam vadanti (Mahā nārayaṇopaniṣad Section 79.7)

Dharma constitutes the foundation of all affairs in the world. People respect those who adhere to Dharma. Dharma insulates (man) against sinful thoughts. Everything in this world is founded on Dharma. Dharma, therefore, is considered supreme.

As noted by HG Wells, Ashoka's name continue to shine even after 2000 years because his ideas of social responsibility are pertinent to our present time. Bruce Rich argues that Ashoka's "essential doctrine" lies in the 'reverence for life': "It is a principle that goes beyond the role of just treatment of human beings of one another: reverence for life means upholding the world." [Bruce Rich: To Uphold the World: A Call for a New Global Ethic from Ancient India, Beacon Press, Boston, MA, USA, 2010]

Ashoka's grandfather, Chandragupta, had an adviser. He was Kautilya, who authored the 4th century BCE book on Economics. It was called Arthaśāstra (Discipline of Material wealth or 'that science which treats of acquiring and maintaining the earth'). Social institutions were constructed to modulate behavior of people through state's oppressive power and by offering economic/fiscal incentives.

A cardinal postulate of a theory of justice is that just behavior had to be complemented by just institutions.

Ashoka tried to introduce his doctrines using a centralized government and using Kautilya's realpolitik of amorality of the state juxtaposed to the proclamation of accumulation of wealth as the chief goal of society. Ashoka's failure is a failure to decentralize decision-making and continued deployment of state power to influence peoples' behavior. Thus, Ashoka failed the harmonization postulate.

Today, the world is witness to what George Soros condemned as 'market fundamentalism'. This is a threat greater than the threat of totalitarian ideology which was demonstrated by the now-dismantled Soviet Union.

113

The key question is: how can achieve a decentralized institutional framework in a transactional society which is getting increasingly globalised and with concentrations of power in select markets.

In Hindu tradition, there are five general principles of conduct or duties: ahimsāsatyāsteyabrahmacaryāparigraha. (Patanjali's *Yogasūtra*, II, 30: numerous editions & translations. Also, in the system Vedānta and elsewhere.)

These are: a) *ahimsā* non-injury towards all creatures; b) *satya* practising truth; c) *asteya* non-stealing; d) *brahmacarya* continence or clean mode of life aiding spiritual development; e) *aparigraha* non-accumulation of all types of possessions or enjoyment of measured life.

The sacredness of earth is attested. 6 whole hymns are adressed to Dyaus-Pṛthivi, 1 to Pṛthivi and there are many references to both of them elsewhere. *Prthiv*i (feminine of Prthu). As *Prthiv*i she is a goddess. *Dyaus* 'Heaven': Greek *Zeus*, Germanic *Tiwaz*. Land or earth is called "*vasudhā*" (=wealth-producing, in *Atharvaveda* and after) and *vasum-dharā* (wealth-holding, in the Upanishads and after); in

114

other words, earth is the store, source or material cause of wealth.

In the Śatapatha Brāhman-a, as a householder settles in his new home and builds the Gārhapatya, the sacred fire-altar, the following description occurs: "Yama hath given the settlement on earth (to this sacrificer); for Yama indeed rules over the settling on this earth, and it is he who grants to this one a settlement on this earth. The Fathers [=deceased ancestors] have prepared this place for him. For Yama is the Kswatra [=nobility or rulingpower] and the Fathers are the clansmen; and to whomever the chief [=Kswatriya], with the approval of the clan, grants a settlement, that settlement is properly given: and in like manner does Yama, the ruling power, with the consent of the Fathers, the clan, now grant to this sacrificer a settlement on this earth." (VII, 1, 1, 3-4)(SBE 5 Vols, 12, 26, 41, 43, 44, transl by J.Eggeling. The square brackets are the author's.) This passage has deep implications. (1) Undoubtedly this principle was in force in the period of the Hymns. (2) The land is a divine entity and belongs to the whole of mankind. It is not just a matter of this generation or this tribe. The land has been prepared by all previous generations, whose spirits are now present in the people of

115

today. Each generation holds the land in custody for the next. (3) The area or district or country is held in common by the whole clan or tribe, community or nation. They, expressing all previous generations, give the land by means of their ruler. (4) The ruler does the giving but he represents Yama, the lord of regulation, King & Judge in the World of Departed Spirits in heaven (Pitrwloka: such is Yama in the Hymns): the land is not really the king's. A Divine Power with the consent of Humanity bestows it through the king on the new settler-sacrificer. (5) The condition is that the receiver will live and work, will settle in the community. (6) More remarkably, nothing is asked in return – other than that the man should settle! And here we have an implicit recognition, which is the loudest declaration, that every man needs land (on which is light, air and space) to live and work. This he should have freely.

This reminds of Plato's allotments in *The Laws*: "Let the apportionment be made with this understanding that the citizen who receives his plot must consider it as common property of the whole State: since this land is his fatherland he should tend it even more diligently than a mother her children – in as much as being a goddess she is mistress over mortals" (740).

The same Brāhmana prohibits the giving away of land in any other way at all. It may not be granted even as a gift to priests who perform sacrifices (or other rituals): " Now of sacrificial gifts. Whatever there is towards the middle of the kingdom other than the land, the men and the property of the brāhmana, of that the eastern region belongs to the Hotṛ... etc" (Hotṛ is a sacrificial priest). Thus land as well as people and the brahmins' property is inalienable. [ŚB XIII, 5, 4, 24 (repeated in XIII, 6, 2, 18) SBE Vol XLIV Delhi, 2nd ed, p402 (and p412).] The same book, a little later, mentions the incident of King Viśvakarman Bhauvana who promised to give land to his officiating priest Kaśyapa. Thereupon Goddess Earth sprang up and reproached him: "No mortal should give me away! Thou wast foolish..."(ŚB XIII, 7, 1, 14-15 (SBE XLVI, p421).) Thus even the king could not give away land as a gift to his priest!

Nārada says : "A householder's house and his field are considered as the two fundamentals of his existence. Therefore let not the king upset either of them; for that is the root of householders." (N, XI, 42.)

Bṛhaspati states : "A privy, a fireplace, a pit or a receptable for leavings of food and other (rubbish), must never be made very close to the house of another man." (Bṛ. XIX, 26. Also Kauṭilya's *Ārthaśāstra*, III, 8.)

Manusmṛti8 ordains: "on all sides of a village (*grāma*: human community) let there be a space-reserve (*parihāra*) of 100 *dhanus* (= about 600 feet) or 3 *śamyā* throws; three times that extend round a town (nagara)". That was the boundary.

"The land shall not be sold for ever: for the land is mine (saith the Lord); for ye (are) strangers and sojourners with Me." Hebrews allowed every family its land holdings (Leviticus, ch 25, 23 ff.)

Upanishad, (Chāndogya Up, IV, 2, 4. Dr Saletore, *Early Indian Economic History*, Bombay, 1973, (p, 459, ch VIII, note 9) refers to Atharvaveda IV, 22, as a petition to the king for a share-grand in a village, But *emaml bhaja grāme* means "give him (ie the ruler!) a share in the village" and not that the king should give land to somebody! It is a prayer to the gods for the prosperity of the ruler (ksratriya, here). King Jānaśruti gives to sage Raikva, gold, cattle, a village and his daughter in mariage. The village is given by the king as a dowry or gift.

Communal possession of land is found in: Lawbooks (Manu VIII, 237; Baudhāyana III, 1, 17). It is restated in Buddhist texts, as well, in Jaimini's Pūrva Mimāmsā (VI, 7, 3), in Jaimini's Pūrva Mimāmsā (VI, 7, 3) a passage in the epic *Mahābhārata* (Bk 14 Aśvamedha: 10,7,...) where the King gives to the sage Vyāsa land but he says this should stay with the King and does not take it! *Rāmāyan-a*, in Bk I Bālakān-dda, ch 13, where again after the *aśvamedha* 'horse-sacrifice, the king wants to give away land to the brahmin-priests but they refused it and said he alone should keep and protect it.

A title (āgama) is stronger than a mere possession (bhoga) and some title is generally needed in order to prove possession (svāmya). However Nārada and Viswn-u (=Vi) favour possession after a lapse of time (N, I 75-82; *Viṣṇu-dharma-śāstra*, V, 187, transl. J. Jolly, SBE, vol VII.), while Yājn[avalkya (=Y) demands a clear title.(Y, II, 29: āgamena viśuddhena bhogo yāti pramānwatām.)

119

Significance of land

A field belongs to the man who first cleared it of wild-growth. (Manu, IX, 44)

Gautama states: "By false evidence concerning small cattle a witness kills ten (of them). Regarding cows, horses, men or land, in each succeeding case (he destroys) ten times as many (as the preceding case). Or regarding land (he destroys) the whole (humanity or world). Hell is the punishment for theft of land. Concerning water (the guilt) is the same as about land"(XIII, 14-18-SBE, II, p 244-5 (Words in brackets are commentators' and translators'). Also Manu,

VIII 98-100.)

Dwellings for new migrants

Baudhāyana says of a *vānaprastha*: "After departing (from his ancestral home), he stops at the extremity of the village, or the boundary, builds there a hut or a cottage and enters it". (III, 1, 17.)

Apastamba: "He shall build a dwelling outside the village with his wife, his children and his (sacred) fires; or he may dwell there alone".(II, 9, 22, 8-9: SBE, II, p 154.)

In Baudhāyana, we find mention of a householder who lives by the mode called "*swannivartan*i", which is a kind of tenant farming. "He cultivates six nivartanas (a nivartana=6000 sq ft) of fallow land giving a share to the owner, or soliciting his permission (to keep the whole produce)." (III, 2, 2,. SBE XIV, p 288. Words in 2nd brackets are not in the original Sanskrit.)

There is also a mode called "*dhruva*" which is a kind of labour for hire for any job.

And here we have perhaps the spermatic forms of hired labour and landlords, of men who do not want the responsibility of having their own farm but prefer to do jobs for others or cultivate other's fields, and of men who do not work themselves their land but hire it to others.

The Buddhist sources present a very mixed situation as regards actual landtenure. There is still common land; the king owns large areas, parts of which he rents out to tenants or gives away as gifts, sometime's only for the duration of a man's life; there are privately owned plots of very large estates which can be rented or sold.(Saletore, pp 661-3. Also F. M. Bongard-Levin, *Mauryan India*, Sterling Publishers, Delhi, 1985,

121

pp 141-3.)

In *Milindapanha* (The Questions of King Milinda or Menander) we find the following statement; "If a man who has cleared land of wood (vana=wood, forest) gets it, people say "this is his land". But the land is not made by him. It is because he has brought the land into use that he is called the lord/master of the land (bhūmisāmiko)".(Both texts are quoted fully in Bongard-Levin, p 141. The Pāli originals are given in notes 132 and 134, pp 215-6. The bracket with *vana* is ours.)

Manu (IX, 44): "Those who know the past know this Earth (pṛthivi) as wife of Pṛthu; they declare a field to belong to whomever cleared it (of wild-growth) and a deer to him who (first pierced it) with a dart."

Kautilya's Arthaśāstra presents private property and royal property in land; there are also vast uninhabited tracts, wastes and jungles, which seem to belong to the State as a whole. These last are used for new settlements (*śunyaniveśa*: settlement or occupation of empty land). Such settlements (forms of colonization) are small or large villages from 100 to 500 families (grāma; II, 1,2).47 Land grants are given to people willing to pay taxes and are,

122

generally, for life only (*aikapuruswika*=fit for one man),
implying that the occupants are tenants, not full owners (II,
1, 8). If they fail to till or to produce adequate quantities
(yes, there are assesors), the plots are taken from them and
given to others (II, 1, 10).

Genesis of private property in land

"It is possible that the rule that all land belongs to the King
reflects an earlier stage in the development of society when
all land was the property of the entire tribe", so writes
Arthaśāstra's editor, Kangle.(*Arthaśāstra*, PtIII, p 171.)
But when "over the generations individual families
continued to hold and till the same separate pieces of land,
a vested interest was created, which practically amounted
to ownership of the separate pieces of land. Then the rights
of alienation came to be recognized".

In stanzas VII, 113–124 Manu delineates: "All that the
villagers should give to the king daily, food, drink, fuel etc,
now the village-master should receive (118). The lord of
the (villages) will enjoy (as much land as suffices for) one
family (*kula*); the lord of 20, five families; the
superintendent of 100 villages, (the revenue from) one
village; the overlord of 1000 villages, that of a town" (119).

All these should be inspected, "For the king's servants who are appointed to protect, generally become rogues who grab the property of others…!"(123)

Manu and the late Dharmaśāstras. Manu states (X, 115) seven legal (*dharmya*) modes of obtaining (*āgama*) wealth (or property: *vitta*): inheritance (*dāya*); finding in the ground or receiving as donation (*lābha*); purchase (*kraya*); conquest (*jaya*: some commentators say "gambling"); lending at interest (*prayoga*); work generally (*karmayoga*); gifts from good people (*sat-pratigraha*). Commentators say that the first three are for all classes; the fourth, for kswatriyas; the fifth and sixth for vaiśyas; the sixth for Śūdras; the seventh for brāhmandas. [Gautama gives almost identical modes of acquisition – inheritance, purchase, seizure etc. (G X, 39-42.)]

Manu's "Of ancient treasurehoards and metals in the ground the king takes half because of protection, for he is the supreme lord-protector of the earth" (VIII 39). Comment on translation: *bhūmer adhipatir hi sah*d has no "(and) because"; it can only be rendered as "for (*hi*) he (*sah*d) is the supreme (*adhi-*) Lord-protector (*-pati*) of the earth (bhūmer)". In other words, the king (*rājā*) takes half share by reason of protection (*raksdandād*) since *he* is the protector – not someone else.

Mitākshara's comments on Yājn[avalkya II, 114, that the sale of a plot takes place only with the consent of a village (*grāma*), relatives and neighbours.(*Mauryan India,* p 146 and 217, n 158.)

"It is quite clear that all unoccupied land is supposed to belong to the king, that is to the state." "Svabhumi used in the sutra 2.24.2 appears to refer to king's personal land. Thus the director of trade (panyadhyaksha) was required to keep separate the produce of king's personal estate (svabhumija) from produce received from 'other places' (parabhumija)... and he had to make different arrangements for their sale. Royal goods (rajapanyah) from king's estte was to be sold at one centre (ekamukham) and goods from other places at many centres (anekamukham)."

In sacrifice Viśvajit, where a king gives away all his possessions, the master of *Mimāmdsā,* Jaimini, makes an exception in sūtra VI, 7, 3: "The land (of the Kingdom) should not be transfered because there should be left some for everyone (or literally, by reason of a remainder for all (Winternitz (vol III, p 511) places Jaimini's sutras in C4th

125

BC, at latest.) : *na bhūmihh syāt sarvān prati avaśiswttatvāt*)". Commentator on Jaimini, Śabaraswāmin, expounds, in Colebrooke's translation: "The monarch has not property on the earth… His kingly power is for government of the realm and extirpation of wrongs; and for that purpose he receives taxes from husbandmen and levies fines from offenders. But right of property is not thereby vested in him… The earth is not the king's but is common to all beings enjoying the fruit of their own labour. It belongs, says Jaimini, to all alike." (Quoted by K P Jayaswal, *Hindu Polity* (1924), Bangalore 1967, pp 331-2, giving Sanskrit text also.)

Nilakantha of C 16th CE says: "Proprietary right in the whole land with regard to villages, lands etc, lies in their respective landlords. The King's right is limited to the collection of tax therefrom. Therefore what is technically called at present "gift of land" etc by the king does not mean giving away of land, but a mere creation of allowance". And Prime Minister Mādhava, also eminent jurist, says: "King's sovereignty is for corecting the wicked and fostering the good. Hence land is not king's wealth. On the other hand, in that land (state-land) there is the common wealth of all living beings to enjoy the fruit of their labour.

Therefore, although there can be a gift of a piece of nonpublic (*asādhāranda*) land, there can be no gift of the Great Land" (Quoted by Jayaswal, pp 332-3, giving Sanskrit text also.).

We can now look at the statement of Bhattttaswāmin, commenting on *Arthaśāstra* II, 24, quoted by Prof Basham (p 110)(Jayaswal's interpretation of this couplet is quite different from ours, taking *Kutṭumbin* as "relative of the King" and not the more usual sense "householder, family-man".) : "The learned see that the king is lord (pati) of land and water; any other thing can be property generally of the people (*kutṭumbin*)." Now, since no authority at all states unequivocally that the King is *the owner of the land* of the country, the interpretation here also must be that the king, as representative of the community, or nation, holds in protective custody, all land and water, both of which cannot (as other things can) become the property of individuals. "pati" is really the lord-protector rather than the lord-proprietor, which would be *svāmin*. (Prof Basham, in fact, cites a Jātaka story where a king tells his mistress that *he cannot give her his kingdom, for he is not its owner!*)

In this light should be seen, too, the king's claim to half of any treasures found in the soil (Manu VIII, 39). A treasure (jewels or metals) in the ground is natural recources, or, in other words, ready products of nature (if a mine), or of other people's labour (if a hoard). It is not a product of the finder's labour, as crops are of farmer's efforts. The treasure belongs to the community (as does the soil). No principle of justice is served if one man obtains it, through luck and not through effort, and thereby gains an advantage over other members of the community. On the contrary, justice would demand that this should be shared by all members of the community. The suprising fact is that the king as custodian of communal goods takes only half, or 1/6 (Manu, VIII, 35), and not more. In fact, Grautama (X, 43) says all "treasure-trove is kingly property" (!) and this sounds a better principle.

VI) The King's (Government's) Function

(a) The coronation Ceremony: the Contract.

"The people (or tribes) elect you to rulership – the five godly regions (or glorious assemblies). Rest thee on the top, the hump (i.e. throne) of the State; thence to us, as mighty-king, distribute wealth".(Atharvaveda III, 4, 2.)

128

This hymn describes, as do many others,(Rgveda X, 173 and 174; Atharvaveda VI, 86 and 87; etc.) the coronation of the King who is elected by the people – or re-elected in some cases.(Atharvaveda III, 3, etc.) The ceremony of the coronation (*Rājasūya*) is highly symbolic.(The details of the Coronation are given in full in the 5th Kānwdwa of *Śatapatha Brāhmanwa*. This part is V, 2, 1, 21.) As the King is led to sit upon the throne he is told:

"This is thy Sovranty (or State)... To thee (it is given) for agriculture, for safekeeping (*kswema*), for wealth, for development". And the narator adds "For welfare (of the people)".(ŚB, V, 2, 1, 21: *iyamw te rāt/...kṛswyai tvā kswemāya tvā rayyai tvā poswāya tvā/* The lines are from *Yajurveda* (White) IX, 22.) The King has already pledged to all the tribes (their representatives), all the classes, all officials (*Ratnin*): "Between the night I was born and the one I shall die,whatever good (*iswttapūrtam-*) I have done, this world and heaven, my life and progeny, may I lose all, if I should injure you".(*Aitareya Brāhmanwa*, VIII, 15.)

The Origin of Kingship (*rājya*) is very ancient. The *Aitareya Brāhmanwa* (I, 14) gives the oldest explanation by means of a tale. It tells how gods and demons were at war and the gods were losing. So they met all together and decided they needed a *rājan* (= king) to lead them: they appointed Soma as king and soon the tide turned in their favour. This is the earliest explanation of the kingly function: an organizer and leader in war selected by his peers, functionaries of State and common people (even metal and wood-workers). (Artharva, III, 5, 6. For more about the origin, see also A.K.Majumdar, *Concise History of Ancient India,* Vol II, *Political Theory...* Munshiram Manoharlal, Delhi, 1983, pp 40, 43.) The story is repeated in *Taittiriya Brāhmanwa* I, 5 (which is later?) with a significant difference. Here the discomfited gods made a sacrifice to highgod Prajāpati (= lord-of-creatures) and he sent his son Indra to become the gods' king.

With this alteration, the king is still a leader in war but now has divine sanction. The second tale involving divine sanction links up with an even earlier and different tradition which does not speak of the origin of kingship as such but of the first or archetypal king Pṛthu. The *Atharvaveda* hymn VIII 10, especially stanza 24, says that Pṛthi (=Pṛthu), son of Vena, extracted out of Virāj (=excellence, majesty, vital-force, the female principle of creation) the art of agriculture and all subsistence for men. At that time

Virāj was moving and mutating and Pṛthu used as his collecting instrument earth herself: this was later said to be the mariage of Earth to Pṛthu whereby she was named also "Pṛthivi". In the epic *Mahābhārata*, VII 69, this tale is elaborated: the earth here is regarded as Pṛthu's daughter that gives to every class of creatures what they want (even poison to the snakes). At no time and in no source is the ruler a priest-king as in other cultures. Yet he is said in *Atharvaveda* XI 5, 17 to protect the kingdom by *brahmacarya* 'continence, chastity' and *tapas* 'spiritual practice, meditation'. This and certain magical rites(66 See J Gonda's 1966 *Ancient Indian Kingship from the Religious Point of View*, Leiden, Brill, pp 65, 71-2, 74-5, 78-9.) that the king should perform indicate that perhaps in remote prehistory king and priest were one person.

Subsequent sources use sometimes the elective process, sometimes the divine sanction. Manu stresses the king's divine aspect; but aware of the danger of despotic tyranny, places the king himself under the jurisdiction of Punishment: "Punishment (*dand- a*) is the King, indeed …the surety for the four orders and the Law (VII, 17)… the king who employs him properly prospers… otherwise gets destroyed by him (27) …He [=Punishment] kills any king

131

who swerves from duty, along with his relatives" (28). *The Arthaśāstra*, the prime authority on secular aspects of Statecraft, gives another story, emphasizing the electoral and contractual idea (I, 13). The same passage states that people must be told that the king performs the function of gods Indra and Yama: that is, he protects by leading (Indra) and by regulating or administering justice (Yama). For this function the people "fixed 1/6 part of the crops, and 1/10 of their goods, and money, as his reward."

The *Sukra-niti-sāra states*: "For the purpose of protection was the King made by the Creator master in form, yet in servitude to the people by means of his sustenance [or, wages: *bhṛti*] which is his own share of their produce" (I, 188).(Quoted in Jayaswal, p 321. It is a late text.)

State (King)

Leading, putting order and protecting: this is the king's function. Even as early as hymn III 43, 5 in the *RV* the king is called *gopā janasya* 'shepherd of the people.' Manu ordains that he should "protect this whole world" (*sarvasya... parirakswanwam*, VII, 2; or just "the whole kingdom"). Nārada, too, sees the King's share of 1/6th of

132

the land's produce as "reward for the protection of his subjects" (VIII, 48).

According to the sage Atri, the king's duties constitute a fivefold sacrifice: "To punish the wicked, to honour the good, to increase the treasury in the right way, to deal impartially with litigants, and to protect the Kingdom (from internal and external enemies) – these five are declared to be sacrifices in the case of the kings".(P. V. Kane, *History of the Dharma-Sā*stras, Poona, 1930-62, Vol, III, p57. The bracket is ours.) Kauṭilya goes a step further: having laid down the duties of different castes (*varn*w*as*), and lifestages (*āśramas*), he states (I, 3, 5, 17), "(The observance of) one's special duty leads to heaven and eternal bliss, but if it is trangressed, people will be exterminated through confusion (of the varnwas and āśramas). Therefore the king must not allow people to transgress their own special duties."

It is noteworthy that Kauṭilya mentions throughout the passage both varnwas and āśramas, emphasizing the goal of supreme beatitude – as in fact do all the Lawbooks.

This is not new of course. In the Hymns the king is expected to give leadership and wealth, or riches (*vasūni*).

But both leadership and wealth can be in the spiritual realm as well. Thus we find in the Brāhmanwas and Upanishads several kings of considerable spiritual attainment, like Janaka of Videha. One very interesting example is King Aśvapati who follows the spiritual path of Self-Knowledge (*ātman-vaiśvānara*);

his fame is such that great Vedic scholars visit him in order to learn from him: and indeed they find that in his kingdom "there is no thief, no drunkard, no miser, no man without the sacred fire, none ignorant and no adulterer or courtesan".(Chāndogya Upaniswat, V, 11, 5-6.)

Obviously the king must protect, encourage and reward spiritual guides, such as brāhmanwas. He (his administration) must provide welfare for those who definitely cannot take care of themselves.(M, VIII, 27-28; Vi III, 6-; G X, 48; etc.) Kauṭilya writes: "The king should provide maintenance for orphans, the aged, the infirm, the helplesss…" etc and he should punish a capable person who abadons his dependants, without provision, even if he does it in order to embrace asceticism (II, 1). Beyond this the king must never shrink from battle; for fighting is the Kswatriya's chief duty. And he must protect his subjects from corupt officials.(M, VII, 87-8 and 121-4; VI III, 43-44 and Y I, 337; etc.) He is to punish anyone who does not remain within the bounds of his own duty (*svadharma*), whatever his position might be, even teacher and priest.(M, VIII, 335; Y I, 357.) Naturally he cannot perform all the administrative functions on his own. So he has to separate the powers and delegate them to good and trusted men who will look after the army, the collection of taxes, and so on, always with a view to the welfare of the whole nation.(M, VII, 60-65.)

Kauṭilya: "In the happiness of his subjects lies the happiness of the King and what is beneficial to them is also his own benefit." (I, 19,34).

Manu says that a "King not-protecting" is one of six persons that people may abandon, like a sinking ship at sea.(BK XI, ch 57 (or 56), 43-45. Also M, IV 61 and G IX, 65.) Manu says as much in X, 113, supported by all his commentators. Where there is deceit, injustice and oppression, there may even follow forcible removal, he implies, even though the king is inviolable and beyond punishment.(VII, 27-8 and III, 2.) "That king who out of folly rashly oppreses the kingdom, soon, together with his relatives, will be deprived of life and kingdom".

The Coronation act and the whole contract is not to be taken lightly. For more information one should consult J Gonda's *Ancient Indian Kingship from the Religious Point of View*, 1966 Leiden, E J Brill.

Environmetal care

The King "should not damage trees that bear fruit or flowers", declares Vaśiṣṭha adding: "He may injure them in order to extend cultivation" (XIX, 11 – 12).

Manu (IX, 279, 281, 285) and others put severe punishments on those who damage water-tanks, reservoirs, dykes and any water-supply, generally; also bridges, temples and other buildings! (Y, II, 278, 297; V, 174. Also *Arthaśāstra* II, 1, 38-39 and III, 8.)

The land should be used fully and be kept in good condition. Manu sets big fines for those who leave rubbish or filth on the highways (IX, 282). Bṛhaspati also lays down fines for those who drop filth, make pits, plant trees or in any way obstruct public passageways (*samdsarana*). He and Nārada extend this prohibition to all public roads,

136

crossroads, sanctuaries of deities and other men's land.(Bṛh XIX 25-29; Nār XI, 15.)

Manu sets big fines for those who leave rubbish or filth on the highways (IX, 282). Bṛhaspati also lays down fines for those who drop filth, make pits, plant trees or in any way obstruct public passageways (samdsarana). He and Nārada extend this prohibition to all public roads, crossroads, sanctuaries of deities and other men's land.(Bṛh XIX 25-29; Nār XI, 15.)

The vaiśyas are encouraged to make profits and increase their wealth "in a righteous way" (dharmen-a=according to law) and be able to provide food for all creatures". (M, IX, 133)

Specialized craftsmen, tradesmen and other occupations, formed guilds and developed their own professional codes. Many law-givers (Ap II, 15, 1; G XI, 20; M VIII, 40-41; etc. EPAI 22) enjoin that these should be respected by the ruler. In fact Yājn[avalkya ordains (I,361) that the king should compel such guilds to comply with their own rules.

Kautilya's *Arthaśāstra* also advocates controls (II, 12ff): mining industries and trade in gold and silver are to be

State monopolies; the government should engage in foreign trade and set up largescale enterprise in liquors, textiles etc.

Moneylending: Manu regards loans etc as sufficiently important and common to assign them under his first of the 18 titles of Law (VIII, 4). He ordains that a money-lender (*vārdhus*wi) can have 1/80 (11/4) interest per month (15% per annum) or even 2% and not become a sinner (*arthakilbis*wi; VIII, 140-1). In the next verse, the interest is increased to 3% for kswatriyas, 4% for vaiśyas and 5% for śūdras. Other lawgivers, including Gautama give very similar percentages.(G XII, 29; V, II, 51; et al.)

Manu: "After due consideration, the king should so always arange the taxes (*kara*) in his realm that both he himself and the performer of work receive their just reward. As the leech, the calf and the bee take their food little by little, even so the king must draw from his realm a moderate annual revenue

(*kara*)"(M, VII, 128-9). This is applied in actual taxes: "After fully considering (the rates of) purchase and sale, the (transport-) distance, (the expense of) food and condiments, the charge of securing the goods and the (eventual) profit, then let the king make the merchants pay tariffs"(M, VII, 127).

The ruler should collect taxes from people in proper time and proper place, in a mild regular form and according to law (*vidhi*).(XII, Śāntiparvan, 38,12) The mild regular form and the law imply that the taxes are known and certain in amount, also, not capricious and arbitrary. In addition, the ruler is advised to consider fully the nature and cost of collecting as well as the amount collected before aranging for such a tax.(XII, Śāntiparvan, 87,16)

Āpastamba makes96 young people liable to tax thus forcing them to enter into the economic game as soon as possible. In other texts tariffs are used to encourage or discourage the traffic of goods into and out of the country: "whatever causes harm to the country and is unnecessary (ie luxury-goods) should be excluded; whatever is highly beneficial as well as rare grain-seeds should be allowed in duty free". (Kauṭilya, II, 16, 21end, 25 etc.)

Taxes. Manu states: "1/50th of cattle and gold is to be taken by the king; of crops1/8th, 1/6th or 1/12th only" (VII, 130).98 Āpastamba maintains a most curious silence on the subject having said that the king's officials should collect the lawful taxes (*Śulka*: in II, 10, 26, 9) and given a long list of persons exempt from taxes (10- 17). But Gautama, refering to other unnamed authorities, gives the 1/50th for cattle and gold; he differs slightly form Manu in giving for crops 1/10th (not 1/12th), 1/8th and 1/6th.

Brahmins, especially *śrotriyas*, i.e. versed in Vedas and sacred lore, are exempt from taxes. So are blind men, idiots, cripples and seventy-year olds.(Manu VIII, 394; et al.) Furthermore, lower-caste people, engaged in small-trade and having a low income, pay a small (*kimcit*) but unspecified tax (Manu VII, 137.) – presumably left to the discretion of the tax-collectors. (This may show concern for marginal production, but just as probably compassion towards poverty.)

In addition to taxes in money-terms, the law-books ordain contribution in workhours – as was practised in feudal Europe. Unskilled men, artisans and śūdras who live by manual labour should work for the State one day per month, says Manu (VIII, 138 and X, 120.) .

Gautama gives the same measure and Vasiswtha probably intends the same with the rule – "(The king) shall take a monthly tax from artisans"(G X, 31; Vas XIX, 28.) .

Manu allows a tax of 25% on produce (X,18). K gives 33% (V,2,2); but when water-taxes and others are added, the amount reaches 50% (even prostitutes pay 50%! – V, 2,23). K considers that the Treasury (*kośa*) is the firm basis of the government (II, 12, 37; VIII, 1, 47-9) and advocates the use of unscrupulous and even criminal methods to collect revenue.

The Vedic sources say very little about taxation. There was definitely a tribute payable to the king called "bali". With regard to this Dr Saletore says, "In the times of the ṛgveda the king was evidently only a kind of guardian expected to protect his subjects and for this protection he was entitled to a payment called *bali*" Saletore, p459. . Sometimes this bali-payment might be excessive for in some hymns it is said that, "the king devours the rich" (*ṛgveda*, I, 65, 4; *Atharva*, IV, 22, 7: but the meaning here may be metaphorical or symbolic). Thus the bali-tax has very ancient origin. (Bali is also a sacrificial offering to gods; also a payment to, or from, religious bodies, like monasteries or priestly authorities. Kauṭilya refers to it as a religious tax in *Arthaśāstra* II, 6. The commentator on Pānini's grammar, (*Aṣṭādhyāyi* II, 1, 36 – on tatpuruswa compounds) in late classical times notes two examples:

Kuberabali, i.e. sacrificial offering to god Kubera; mahārājabali offering or payment to the king or emperor.)

Arthaśāstra II, 1, ff. It concerns the granting of land to new settlers. The chief Collector (*samāhartṛ*) maintains through assessor-assistants a record of all agricultural holdings showing the various grades of fields (fertility and irigation and nature of crops raised in them). If the settlers do not cultivate the land, or do not cultivate it well, and therefore do not produce enough, they shall lose their land to others – and shall make good the loss of taxes to the State.

Land-value taxation

Manu has an *atyaya* levy which is a payment (tax or fine) to the State according to an original valuation, when there is loss (*atyaya*) of produce due to the cultivator's negligence.

Āpastamba's rule states: "If a person who has taken (a lease of) land (for cultivation) does not exert himself, and hence (the land) bears no crop, he shall, if he is rich, be made to pay (to the owner of the land the value of the crop) that ought to have grown" (II, 2, 28, 1). Olivelle's translation reads; "If someone takes a piece of land on lease and it produces no harvest because he puts no effort in it, then if he has the means, he should be made to pay the landowner what would have been his due": here the distinctions between original sūtra and later commentary have been removed quite arbitrarily, the "landlord" *kswetraswāmin* being inserted from the scholiasts. The words in brackets are not in the original but are supplied by the translator who follows the explanations of commentators. This rendering gives a rule (crop-sharing) that certainly applied to many regions right up to India's Independence, and undoubtedly applies to other agricultural less-developed countries. But there is no need to limit the rule only to such a situation – the sharing of crops between landlord and tenant. Manu has a similar rule with respect to default of-tax-payments, just like Kauṭilya's.

Manu's rule states: "If (the crops are destroyed by) the husbandman's fault, the fine shall amount to ten times as much as the king's share; but the fine (shall be) only half that amount if (the fault lay) with the servants and the farmer had no knowledge of it" (VIII, 243). The bracketed words, again inserted by the translator, are justified here by the preceding and subsequent stanzas. The rule concerns loss of tax; therefore the cultivator must pay a fine. Thus land cannot be held idle but must be used to full capacity.

Stripped of the additions, Āpastamba's rule reads: "*If any person holding land does not exert himself and hence bears no produce, he shall, if rich, be made to pay what ought to have been produced.*" We are fully entitled to stay with the original for the main commentator here is Haradatta who (according to Olivelle, following P.V. Kane) lived at C1100-1300CE, that is at least 1500 if not 3000 years later. Then, the sūtra itself

*ks*wetram- *parigṛhyotthānābhāvāt phalābhāve yat samṛddhas sa bhavi tad apahāryah*h makes perfectly good sense as it stands and as here translated without need of insertions from the commentators who, as is often the case, understand the original no better than modern scholars. The lack of understanding is due, it seems, to the confusion generated by the subsequent emergence of feudal conditions (V d above) and the like, and by the consequent loss of clearly defined and remembered principles, like the ones we describe.

Before closing we ought to examine a passage in Gautama, which has considerable interest. Having given four rules for different taxes (rates and goods), sūtras 24-27 of chapter X, and the duty of the king to protect the taxpayer and give particular attention to the collection of taxes, 28-29, Gautama adds provocatively: "He (i.e. the king) shall live on the surplus (*adhikena vṛttih*h)."

What is this "surplus" (=*adhika*)? Some take this to mean: "The king shall live on taxes paid for additional occupations exercised by him". Others explain: "The king shall live on the surplus which remains, after providing for the external and internal security of the kingdom". The latter interpretation seems more logical and probable, certainly. But in that case one would expect the use of the word "remainder" (*śeswa*) rather than "additional" (*adhika*). I would suggest a third possibility. The "surplus" is the difference between the less and more productive plots, that is the surplus produce, which, in modern terms, is the economic rent or surplus value. This may sound far-fetched, but only because our thinking has been conditioned by the arbitrary tax-rates 1/6th, 1/8th etc, given repeatedly in the sources. In fact this is more reasonable. A wise lawgiver would ordain that the rich on the more productive sites should pay out of their surplus for the king's (and his administration's) expenses, not the poorer,

145

who would thereby become even poorer and would need help. As we saw, Āpastamba makes a similar distinction.

Although, there is little else in the sources to support this view, yet this rule must refer to a very old situation when there were not many taxes but only the one contribution to the king (the Vedic bali), the wages for his maintenance as reward for the protection he offered. The other taxes are later inventions, and they are all variations and precursors of our modern and most dear income tax.

Śreṇi dharma: coping with greed and corruption

For nearly 3000 years since 800 BCE and perhaps earlier, *śreṇi* has been the corporate form of varṇa system of social organization -- *varṇāśrama dharma* -- in Hindu industrial, arts, crafts, business and civic entities. This *śreṇi* corporate form pre-dates the earliest proto-Roman corporations; *śreṇi* was widespread in Ancient India in business, social and civic activities; this corporate form continues to exist even today in Independent India, despite the adoption of a written Constitution governed by principles of Roman jurisprudence and laissez-faire economic principles governing the wealth of the nation. Indian ethical pluralism is called *dharma* ; *śreṇi dharma* is *dharma* applicable to a corporation. The laws governing *śreṇi* are called *śreṇi dharma* , emphasizing social responsibility of corporations. *śreṇi dharma* provides the mechanism to embed 'social ethic' enhancing the corporate model of capitalism or socialism either of which operates within the framework of 'rational, materialistic economic ethos'. Hindu society attaches importance to ethical values, *ātman* (innate cosmic energy) as also to the

147

creation of wealth of a nation. An ascetic is as respected in Hindu society as a just ruler of a state. This remarkable integration of materialistic ethos with the social ethic is unique in the story of human civilizations. *śreṇi dharma* as social capital can supply the missing element of trusteeship. This *śreṇi dharma* constitutes an impressive contribution of Hindu civilization to economic thought, adding spiritual value to materialistic ethos.

In Maslow's (1943) hierarchy or pyramid of human physiological needs which are at the bottom to the need of self-actualization which is at the pinnacle, the expectation is that every member of a corporation will be motivated and resolve to reach the pinnacle, up the ladder. This resolution has to be a vow, a dedication in the process of understanding the essential unity of the *ātman* (spark from the divine) with the*paramātman* (the supreme divine).

In the tradition of Indian Ocean civilizations, this unity is *dharma -dhamma*, the eternal, ethical ordering principle.

A modern *śreṇi* can evolve into a *dharma* corporation, exemplifying economic justice in a moral order.

A facet of dharma-dhamma to combat greed which is the root cause of corruption is śreṇi dharma which can be elaborated as social ethic, social insurance and social capital which

- [ ] supplies the missing element – of *dāna,* 'giving, liberality'-- in the economic progress imperative,

- [ ] dramatically mitigates the deleterious effect of greed resulting in misappropriation of wealth created by economic progress,

- [ ] obviates the need for state-sponsored regulation or interventions, and

- [ ] results in a socially responsible corporate form as an economic engine.

Re-adoption of the millennial old śreṇi dharma will manadate the reform and amendment of company law by incorporation of a *śreṇi dharma* clause in the articles of association. This clause should specify a percentage, say 5 to 10 per cent of the turnover of a corporation to be accumulated into and spent as *śreṇi dharma* fund for social causes, beyond the core business of the corporation. By making the operations of the fund auditable and subject to public scrutiny through financial sentinels such as

149

regulators of the marketplace, a legally binding process can be achieved, by adding the spiritual value of ethical responsibility to the financial balance sheet of a corporation. The Chairperson and Board of Directors of such a corporation incorporating *śreṇi dharma* will be responsible to make disclosures in their annual reports to shareholders the contributions made into and outgo from the *śreṇi dharma* fund. The fault-line of *lobha*, 'greed', will be gradually jumped with such mandated provisions of incorporation, periodical reporting to share-holders and voluntary enforcement of the provisions by the officers of a modern *śreṇi*.

Modern high-growth sectors like the Information Technology (IT) sector should include a clause of incorporation which can be called *śreṇi dharma* .Such an incorporation will help incorporate in a fast-growing technology sector of the economy of the world the ethic of social responsibility. There is evidence that many SSI clusters continue to be governed by written trust deeds (in Sanskrit, *śreṇi dharma* or in Tamil, *aṟakkaṭṭaḷai* – the *dharma* statute). This form of incorporation can be extended to large scale or global level industry or enterprise. One reason why this salutary form has not been introduced is the excessive reliance on Roman jurisprudence with emphasis on individual rights without a corresponding emphasis on social responsibility and duty of a corporate entity. The deficiency can be remedied by calling for a mandatory incorporation clause stipulating a pre-determined percentage of the turnover of an incorporated corporation to be set aside as social security and as social capital to be exclusively used for social welfare.

śreṇi dharma is a voluntary and spontaneous fulfillment of social ethic of a corporation in a polity. *śreṇi dharma* , a unique contribution to economic thought and practice, should reform corporations world-wide – to jump the fault-lines of greed, corruption and excesses of state or corporate power while adding value to materialistic ethos, upgrading the joy of material living to ecstasy of being and sharing as bliss.

The acceptance of *śreṇi dharma* in Indian Ocean Community, as one of the youngest nations on the globe (accounting for 70% of the population as less than 35 years of age), will result in a paradigm shift introducing social ethic in global economic thought and practice. Acceptance may involve reforms in Companies Act or Memoranda of Association or Incorporation of Companies, with specific, non-fuzzy ethical rules such as an agreement to set apart 5 to 10% of the income of a corporation for social causes. The enforcement of the rules has to be voluntary and by the corporation itself. The corporate tribunals will judge the deviant behavior from the agreed ethical norms and social responsibilities including specifications of punishment for disregard of the rules and procedures for legal redress by appeal against the verdict, say, of a *śreṇi* tribunal.

A rich civilizational tradition that Indian Ocean Community represents – in the comity of nations -- is destined to contribute to economic justice in a sustainable, global, moral order.

As Indian Ocean Community, free from colonial domination, emerges as a global economic power, it is time to recognize and reinstate *śreṇi dharma*, or social capital, as the missing element of economics to create, nurture and enhance the wealth of nations, while making *śreṇi dharma* an integral part of modern economic paradigm.

With dharma, yes, we can. We can be the agents of change of the world economy, reaching out to the unreached, endeavoring to achieve the ethical imperative: *sarve bhavantu sukhinah* (let all beings be happy) (ādi śankarācārya).

Hrishikesh Vinod, who edited a Handbook of Hindu Economic Thought (which includes an article on *śreṇi dharma* by S. Kalyanaraman) referred to an interesting article of Max H. Bazerman and Ann E. Tenbrunsel (2011) which discussed lapses in behavioral ethics – among regulators, prosecutors, auditors, journalists -- caused, sometimes, by their self-interest to protect reputation of corporate clients. Bazerman and Tenbrunsel make a fine distinction between such willful actions or ignorance. Maybe it is human nature to condone such lapses, but the organizational structure should provide for honest discussions within a corporation about ethical transgressions which result in excessive greed. The structure and function of Hindu corporate form has shown how a commitment can be achieved by corporate clients and regulators alike by setting up a standard percentage of *śreṇi dharma*. This overarching corporate ethic with built-in behavioral ethic expected from all corporate actors and incorporation of this mandatory social welfare contribution in the memorandum of incorporation will help mitigate the effects of excessive greed.

A monograph is presented in three sections:

1. Evolution of *śreṇi dharma as* social corporate statute over 3 millennia;

2. Economics of *śreṇi* as ethical cure for *lobha*, 'greed';

3. Incorporation of Hindu *śreṇi* in economic thought and practice.

Śreṇi dharma can be operationalised by reform steps of the type suggested by the late Rajaji:

"Fate of the nation is doomed if corruption poisons its life in very sphere, as most people feel and complain that it does today in our land. Administration at all levels, the economic controls which the Government exercises over those engaged in production and distribution, the transport service by road, rail and air, the elections that are held to recruit persons to the various public bodies from the villages up to Delhi, these and other public activities are poisoned with this fatal poison, and the process is so widely prevalent that people seem reconciled to it. Democracy is disclosing itself as a puppet dancing to the pull of money-strings. It is painful having to say all this about one's own country, one's own people and one's own administration. But the evil cannot be got rid of by being un-confessed and our sufferings borne in silence.

"Human nature cannot tolerate this state of affairs. The crisis will lead to revolution of some kind, communist or fascist or military. The people have to face this corruption on one side and high prices and unbearable tax-levies on the other. Oppression and corruption must lead to revolt, and passing through anarchy, democracy must turn into dictatorship. Neither can the resulting tyranny escape the total evil of the times. The dictatorship will not be a relief, for that, too, will be corrupt.

"The only hope for the nation lies in the possibility of restoring good government. The interference of ministers and others with legitimate and illegitimate powers derived from so called democracy has transformed a fairly good government (of 1950s) into an intolerably bad administrative machine. Can we retrace the steps and secure an improvement in the morale of our administrative machinery? I believe we can. Let us hope we can secure a dedicated set of young people to join the service ranks in all departments through whom we can get this revolution of

155

character accomplished. In order to hope for this, we should make sure of a few things besides appealing to intelligent youth to dedicate them selves to a holy war against corruption.

"We must elevate the simple life to the status it had enjoyed in Gandhian and pre-independence days. It is the 'standard of life' that has corrupted and is corrupting our souls.

"We should make administration less expensive by reducing the number of people engaged in that unproductive but important work, while at the same time paying adequate salaries to those employed.

"The development of productive industries, should be unhampered by controls and bureaucratic hurdles, so that they may grow quickly and absorb more and more of intelligent young men instead of their being driven by necessity to government service.

"Less taxation and less inflation, abandonment of wholly wrong plan of finding industrial capital by oppressive taxation, and release of private capital and private initiative

from the barbed wire entanglement of Central planning –
these will help to a large extent in clearing the air of the
poisonous fog of corruption.

"There is hope if the young men and women of our country
vow to live simply, and to be honest under any
circumstances and in any employment. Education is of no
use if this dedicated spirit does not crown the acquisition of
useful knowledge. Rectitude and rectitude only can save us.
Hope thus rests on the restoration of faith in God, and even
this must be given by Him. May He give us that faith in His
mercy and enable us to save our dear motherland, which
does not fate that over-hangs it."

Rāṣṭram -State-Panchayat structure for a dharma-dhamma
constitution

Rāṣṭram is the path which led the ancestors of present-day
Indians to move into Indian Ocean region to present the
realization of janapadas and organization of the state,
governed by dharma, the global ethic.

Within this all-enveloping framework, dharma as applied to
governance, called rajadharma is explained as the
facilitation of individuals of the samajam attaining the
purushartha of dharma, artha and kaama without

157

transgressing dharma, the ethical principles of conduct and inter-personal relationships. This is affirmed by Barhaspatya sutra, II-43-44: "The goal of rajaniti (polity) is the accomplishment of dharma, artha, kāma. Artha and kāma must be subject to the test of dharma. Dharma was supreme law of the state and rulers and subjects alike were subservient to this law. Dharma is the constitutional law of modern parlance, explaining the contours of the functions and responsibilities of the state, constraining the ruler by regulations which restrain the exercise of sovereignty by the ruler – a parallel to the paradigm of checks and balances enshrined in modern constitutions to prevent abuse of power while ensuring equal protection to the subjects without discrimination. "Just as the mother Earth gives an equal support to all the be living, a king must give support to all without no discrimination." (Manusmruti). "The king must furnish protection to associations following ordinances of the Veda (Naigamas) which non-believers (pāṣaṇḍi) and to others as well." (*Naradasmruti, Dharmakos'a*, p. 870). In Indonesia also, she is known as *Ibu Pertiwi* ('Mother Earth').

Upholding the earth for wealth

Varāha avatār of Viṣṇu upholding the earth. Sculpture in Udayagiri, cave 5, wall relief, ca 400-450 CE

Many ancient texts provide for lucid economic analyses which provide perspectives relevant for an economic theory.

A two-thousand year old work is *Thirukkural* in Tamil which provides a framework for some fundamental axioms which relate to a theory of wealth.

குறள் 256

திணற்பொருட்டால் கொல்லா துலகெனின்
யாரும்
விலைப்பொருட்டால் ஊன்றருவா ரில்

Thinarporuttaal Kollaadhu Ulakenin Yaarum
Vilaipporuttaal Oondraruvaa Ril

'We eat the slain,' you say, by us no living creatures die;
Who'd kill and sell, I pray, if none came there the flesh to buy

குறள் 361

அவாவென்ப எல்லா உயிர்க்குமெஞ் ஞான்றுந்
தவாஅப் பிறப்பீனும் வித்து

Avaaenpa Ellaa Uyirkkum Enj Gnaandrum
Thavaaap Pirappeenum Viththu

The wise declare, through all the days, to every living
thing

That ceaseless round of birth from seed of strong desire
doth spring

குறள் 368

அவாவில்லார்க் கில்லாகுந் துன்பம்.

துண்டேல்

தவாஅது மேன்மேல் வரும்

Avaaillaark Killaakun Thunpam Aqdhuntel
Thavaaadhu Menmel Varum

Affliction is not known where no desires abide;
Where these are, endless rises sorrow's tide

Bhu-Sukta of Rigveda: *Oh Goddess Aditi, You pervade
the earth,*

*You are supreme in heaven, You are vast in the
environment,*

*I place on your lap, oh Aditi, Fire, the food giver for
eating of food.*

Prithvī-Sukta: Hymn to the Earth (Atharva Veda)

सत्यं बृहदृतमुग्रं दीक्षा तपो ब्रह्म यज्ञः पृथिवीं धारयन्ति ।
सा नो भूतस्य भव्यस्य पत्न्युरुं लोकं पृथिवी नः कृणोतु ॥१॥

असंबाधं मध्यतो मानवानां यस्या उद्वतः प्रवतः समं बहु ।
नानावीर्या ओषधीर्या बिभर्ति पृथिवी नः प्रथतां राध्यतां नः ॥२॥

Truth, high and potent Law, the Consecrating Rite,

Fervour, Brahma, and Sacrifice uphold the Earth.

May she, the Queen of all that is and is to be, may

Prithivī make ample space and room for us. ‖ 1

Not overcome by the crowd of Manu's sons, she who

hath many heights and floods and level plains;

She who bears plants endowed with many varied powers,

may Prithivī for us spread wide and favour us. ‖ 2

यस्यां समुद्र उत सिन्धुरापो यस्यामन्नं कृष्टयः संबभूवुः ।
यस्यामिदं जिन्वति प्राणदेजत्सा नो भूमिः पूर्वपेये दधातु ॥३॥

यस्याश्चतस्रः प्रदिशः पृथिव्या यस्यामन्नं कृष्टयः संबभूवुः ।
या बिभर्ति बहुधा प्राणदेजत्सा नो भूमिर्गोष्वप्यन्ने दधातु ॥४॥

यस्यां पूर्वे पूर्वजना विचक्रिरे यस्यां देवा असुरानभ्यवर्तयन् ।
गवामश्वानां वयसश्च विष्ठा भगं वर्चः पृथिवी नो दधातु ॥५॥

विश्वंभरा वसुधानी प्रतिष्ठा हिरण्यवक्षा जगतो निवेशनी ।
वैश्वानरं बिभ्रती भूमिरग्निमिन्द्रऋषभा द्रविणे नो दधातु ॥६॥

यां रक्षन्त्यस्वप्ना विश्वदानीं देवा भूमिं पृथिवीमप्रमादम् ।
सा नो मधु प्रियं दुहामथो उक्षतु वर्चसा ॥७॥

यार्णवेऽधि सलिलमग्र आसीद्यां मायाभिरन्वचरन्मनीषिणः ।
यस्या हृदयं परमे व्योमन्त्सत्येनावृतममृतं पृथिव्याः ।
सा नो भूमिस्त्विषिं बलं राष्ट्रे दधात्तुत्तमे ॥८॥

यस्यामापः परिचराः समानीरहोरात्रे अप्रमादं चरन्ति ।
सा नो भूमिर्भूरिधारा पयो दुहामथो उक्षतु वर्चसा ॥९॥

In whom the sea, and Sindhu, and the waters, in whom our
food and corn-lands had their being,
In whom this all that breathes and moves is active, this
Earth, assign us foremost rank and station! || 3

She who is Lady of the earth's four regions, in whom our food and corn-lands had their being,

Nurse in each place of breathing, moving creatures, this Earth, vouchsafe us kine with milk that fails not! || 4

On whom the men of old before us battled, on whom the Gods attacked the hostile demons,

The varied home of bird, and kine and horses, this Prithivī, vouchsafe us luck and splendour! || 5

Firm standing-place, all-bearing, store of treasures, gold-breasted, harbourer of all that moveth.

May Earth who bears Agni Vaisvānara, Consort of mighty Indra, give us great possessions || 6

May Earth, may Prithivī, always protected with ceaseless care by Gods who never slumber,

May she pour out for us delicious nectar, may she bedew us with a flood of splendour. || 7

She who at first was water in the ocean, whom with their wondrous powers the sages followed,

May she whose heart is in the highest heaven, compassed about with truth, and everlasting,

May she, this Earth, bestow upon us lustre, and grant us power in loftiest dominion. || 8

On whom the running universal waters flow day and night
with never-ceasing motion,

May she with many streams pour milk to feed us, may
she bedew us with a flood of splendour. ‖ 9

यामु॒श्विना॒वमि॑माता॒ं विष्णु॒र्य॑स्यां विच॒क्रमे॑   ।
इन्द्रो॒ यां च॒क्र आत्म॒ने॑ऽनमि॒त्रां श॒ची॑प॒तिः   ।
सा नो॒ भूमि॑र्वि॑ सृ॑जतां मा॒ता पु॒त्राय॑ मे॒ पय॑ः   ‖१०‖

गि॒र॒य॒स्ते॒ पर्व॑ता हि॒मव॑न्तोऽर॒ण्यं ते॑ पृ॒थिवि॑ स्यो॒नम॑स्तु   ।
बभ्रुं॑ कृ॒ष्णां रो॒हि॑णीं वि॒श्वरू॑पां ध्रु॒वां भूमिं॑ पृथि॒वीमि॑न्द्र॒ग॑प्ताम्   ।

She whom the Asvins measured out, o'er whom the foot
of Vishnu strode,

Whom Indra, Lord of Power and Might, freed from all
foemen for himself,

May Earth pour out her milk for us, a mother unto me her
son. ‖ 10

O Prithivī, auspicious be thy woodlands, auspicious be thy
hills and snow-clad mountains.

Unslain, unwounded, unsubdued, I have set foot upon
the Earth,

On earth brown, black, ruddy and every-coloured, on the
firm earth that Indra guards from danger. ‖ 11

165

अजीतोऽहतो अन्नतोऽध्यष्ठां पृथिवीमहम् ॥११॥

यत्ते मध्यं पृथिवि यद्व नभ्यं यास्त ऊर्जस्तन्व [ः संबभूवुः ।
तासु नो धेह्यभि नः पवस्व माता भूमिः पुत्रो अहं पृथिव्याः ।
पर्जन्यः पिता स उ नः पिपर्तु ॥१२॥

यस्यां वेदिं परिगृह्णन्ति भूम्यां यस्यां यज्ञं तन्वते विश्वकर्माणः ।
यस्यां मीयन्ते स्वरवः पृथिव्यामूर्ध्वाः शुक्रा आहृत्याः पुरस्तात् ।
सा नो भूमिर्वर्धयद्वर्धमाना ॥१३॥

यो नो द्वेषत्पृथिवि यः पृतन्याद्योऽभिदासान्मनसा यो वधेन ।
तं नो भूमे रन्धय पूर्वकृत्वरि ॥१४॥

त्वज्जातास्त्वयि चरन्ति मर्त्यास्त्वं बिभर्षि द्विपदस्त्वं चतुष्पदः ।
तवेमे पृथिवि पञ्च मानवा येभ्यो ज्योतिरमृतं मर्त्येभ्य उद्यन्त्सूर्यो
रश्मिभिरातनोति ॥१५॥

ता नः प्रजाः सं दुहतां समग्रा वाचो मधु पृथिवि धेहि मह्यम् ॥१६॥

विश्वस्वं [मातरमोषधीनां ध्रुवां भूमिं पृथिवीं धर्मणा धृताम् ।
शिवां स्योनामनु चरेम विश्वहा ॥१७॥

O Prithivī, thy centre and thy navel, all forces that have
issued from thy body

Set us amid those forces; breathe upon us. I am the son
of Earth, Earth is my Mother.

Parjanya is my Sire; may he promote me. || 12

Earth on whose surface they enclose the altar, and all-
performers spin the thread of worship;

166

In whom the stakes of sacrifice, resplendent, are fixed and
raised on high before the oblation,

may she, this Earth, prospering, make us prosper. || 13

The man who hates us, Earth, who fights against us,
who threaten us with thought or deadly weapon, make him
our thrall as thou hast done aforetime. || 14

Produced from thee, on thee move mortal creatures:
thou bearest them, both quadruped and biped.
Thine, Prithivī, are these Five human Races, for whom,
though mortal, Sūrya as he rises spreads with his rays the
light that is immortal. || 15

In concert may these creatures yield us blessings. With
honey of discourse, O Earth, endow me. || 16

Kind, ever gracious be the Earth we tread on, the firm
Earth, Prithivī, borne up by Order, mother of plants and
herbs, the all-producer. || 17

मुहत्सधस्थं महती बंभूविथ मुहान्वेगं एजथुर्वेपथुष्टे ।
मुहांस्त्वेन्द्रो रचत्यप्रमादम् ।
सा नों भूमे प्र रोचयु हिरुययस्येव संदृशि मा नों द्विचतु कश्चन ॥१८॥

अग्निर्भूम्यामोषधीष्वग्निमापो बिभ्रत्यग्निरश्मसु ।
अग्निरन्तः पुरुषेषु गोष्वश्वेष्वग्नयः ॥१९॥

167

A vast abode hast thou become, the Mighty. Great stress is on thee, press and agitation, but with unceasing care great Indra guards thee.

So make us shine, O Earth, us with the splendour of gold. Let no man look on us with hatred. || 18

Agni is in the earth, in plants; the waters hold Agni in them, in the stones is Agni.

Agni abideth deep in men: Agnis abide in cows and steeds. || 19

अग्निर्दिव आ तपत्यमेर्देवस्योर्वंश्वन्तरिक्षम् ।
अग्निं मर्तास इन्धते हव्यवाहं घृतप्रियम् ॥२०॥

अग्निर्वासाः पृथिव्यसितञ्जूस्त्विषीमन्तं संशितं मा कृणोतु ॥२१॥

भूम्यां देवेभ्यो ददति यज्ञं हव्यमरंकृतम् ।
भूम्यां मनुष्या जीवन्ति स्वधयान्नेन मर्त्याः ।
सा नो भूमिः प्राणमायुर्दधातु जरदष्टिं मा पृथिवी कृणोतु ॥२२॥

यस्ते गन्धः पृथिवि संबभूव यं बिभ्रत्योषधयो यमापः ।
यं गन्धर्वा अप्सरसश्च भेजिरे तेन मा सुरभिं कृणु मा नो द्विक्षत कश्चन ॥२३॥

यस्ते गन्धः पुष्करमाविवेश यं संजभ्रुः सूर्याया विवाहे ।
अमर्त्याः पृथिवि गन्धमग्रे तेन मा सुरभिं कृणु मा नो द्विक्षत कश्चन ॥२४॥

यस्ते गन्धः पुरुषेषु स्त्रीषु पुंसु भगो रुचिः ।
यो अश्वेषु वीरेषु यो मृगेषु हस्तिषु ।
कन्यायां वर्चो यद्भूमि तेनास्माँ अपि सं सृज मा नो द्विक्षत कश्चन ॥२५॥

Agni gives shine and heat in heaven: the spacious air is his, the God's

Lover of fatness, bearer of oblation, men enkindle him. || 20

Dark-kneed, invested with a fiery mantle, Prithivī sharpen me and give me splendour! || 21

On earth they offer sacrifice and dressed oblation to the Gods.
Men, mortals, live upon the earth by food in their accustomed way.
May that Earth grant us breath and vital power. Prithivī give me life of long duration! || 22

Scent that hath risen from thee, O Earth, the fragrance which growing herbs and plants and waters carry,
Shared by Apsarases, shared by Gandharvas therewith make thou me sweet: let no man hate me. || 23

Thy scent which entered and possessed the lotus, the scent which they prepared at Sūryā's bridal,
Scent which Immortals Earth! of old collected, therewith make thou me sweet: let no man hate me. || 24

Thy scent in women and in men, the luck and light that is in males, that is in heroes and in steeds in sylvan beasts and elephants,

The splendid energy of maids, therewith do thou unite us, Earth! Let no man look on us with hate. || 25

शिला भूमिरश्मा पांसुः सा भूमिः संधृता धृता ।
तस्यै हिरण्यवचसे पृथिव्या अकरं नमः ॥२६॥

यस्यां वृक्षा वानस्पत्या ध्रुवास्तिष्ठन्ति विश्वहा ।
पृथिवीं विश्वधायसं धृतामुच्छावर्दामसि ॥२७॥

Rock earth, and stone, and dust, this Earth is held together, firmly bound.
To this gold-breasted Prithivī mine adoration have I paid. || 26

Hither we call the firmly held, the all-supporting Prithivī,
On whom the trees, lords of the wood, stand evermore immovable. || 27

उदीराणा उतासीनास्तिष्ठन्तः प्रक्रामन्तः ।
पुद्धां दक्षिणसव्याभ्यां मा व्यथिष्महि भूम्याम् ॥२८॥

विमृग्वरीं पृथिवीमा वदामि त्वमां भूमिं ब्रह्मणा वावृधानाम् ।
ऊर्जं पुष्टं बिभ्रतीमन्नभागं घृतं त्वाभि नि षीदेम भूमे ॥२९॥

शुद्धा न आपस्तन्वे ् चरन्तु यो नः सेदुरप्रिये तं नि दध्मः ।
पवित्रेण पृथिवि मोत्पुनामि ॥३०॥

यास्ते प्राचीः प्रदिशो या उदीचीर्यास्ते भूमे अधराद्याश्च पश्चात् ।
स्योनास्ता मह्यं चरते भवन्तु मा नि पप्तं भुवने शिश्रियाणः ॥३१॥

मा नः पश्चान्मा पुरस्तान्नुदिष्ठा मोत्तरादधरादुत ।
स्वस्ति भूमे नो भव मा विदन्परिपन्थिनो वरीयो यावया वधम् ॥३२॥

यावन्तेऽभि विपश्यामि भूमे सूर्येण मेदिना ।
तावन्मे चक्षुर्मा मेष्टोत्तरामुत्तरां समाम् ॥३३॥

यच्छयानः पर्यावर्ते दक्षिणं सव्यमभि भूमे पार्श्वम्
उत्तानास्त्वा प्रतीचीं यत्पृष्टीभिरधिशेमहे ।
मा हिंसीस्तत्रै नो भूमे सर्वस्य प्रतिशीवरि ॥३४॥

Sitting at ease or rising up, standing or going on our way.
With our right foot and with our left we will not reel upon
the earth. || 28

I speak to Prithivī the purifier, to patient Earth who
groweth strong through Brahma.
O Earth, may we recline on thee who bearest strength,
increase, portioned share of food, and fatness. || 29

Purified for our bodies flow the waters: we bring distress on him who would attack us.

I cleanse myself, O Earth, with that which cleanseth. || 30

Earth, be thine eastern and thy northern regions, those lying southward and those lying westward.

Propitious unto me in all my movements. Long as I tread the ground let me not stumble. || 31

Drive us not from the west or east, drive us not from the north or south,

Be gracious unto us, O Earth: let not the robbers find us; keep the deadly weapon far away. || 32

Long as, on thee, I look around, possessing Sūrya as a friend,

So long, through each succeeding year, let not my power of vision fail. || 33

When, as I lie, O Earth, I turn upon my right side and my left,

When stretched at all our length we lay our ribs on thee who meetest us.

Do us no injury there, O Earth who furnishest a bed for all. || 34

यत्ते भूमे विखनामि क्षिप्रं तदपि रोहतु ।
मा ते मर्म विमृग्वरि मा ते हृदयमर्पिपम् ॥३५॥

ग्रीष्मस्ते भूमे वर्षाणि शरद्धेमन्तः शिशिरो वसन्तः ।
ऋतवस्ते विहिता हायनीरंहोरात्रे पृथिवि नो दुहाताम् ॥३६॥

Let what I dig from thee, O Earth, rapidly spring and
grow again.

O Purifier, let me not pierce through thy vitals or thy heart.
‖ 35

Earth, may thy summer, and thy rains, and autumn, thy
winter, and thy dewy frosts, and spring-time.

May thy years, Prithivī! and ordered seasons, and day
and night pour out for us abundance. ‖ 36

यापे सर्पं विजमाना विमृग्वरी यस्यामासन्नग्नयो ये अप्स्वऽन्तः ।
परा दस्यून्ददती देवपीयूनिन्द्रं वृणाना पृथिवी न वृत्रम् ।
शक्राय दध्रे वृषभाय वृष्णे ॥३७॥

यस्यां सदोहविर्धाने यूपो यस्यां निमीयते ।
ब्रह्माणो यस्यामर्चन्त्यृग्भिः साम्रा यजुर्विदः ।
युज्यन्ते यस्यामृत्विजः सोममिन्द्राय पातवे ॥३८॥

यस्यां पूर्वे भूतकृत ऋषयो गा उदानृचुः ।
सप्त सत्रेण वेधसो यज्ञेन तपसा सह ॥३९॥

सा नो भूमिरा दिशतु यद्धनं कामयामहे ।
भगो अनुप्रयुङ्क्तामिन्द्र एतु पुरोगवः ॥४०॥

यस्यां गायन्ति नृत्यन्ति भूम्यां मर्त्या व्यैलबाः ।
युध्यन्ते यस्यामाक्रन्दो यस्यां वदति दुन्दुभिः ।
सा नो भूमिः प्र णुदतां सपत्नानसपत्नं मा पृथिवी कृणोतु ॥४१॥

यस्यामन्नं व्रीहियवौ यस्या इमाः पञ्च कृष्टयः ।
भूम्यै पर्जन्यपत्न्यै नमोऽस्तु वर्षमेदसे ॥४२॥

The purifier, shrinking from the Serpent, she who held fires
that lie within the waters,

Who gives as prey the God-blaspheming Dasyus, Earth
choosing Indra for her Lord, not Vritra, hath clung to
Sakra, to the Strong and Mighty. ‖ 37

Base of the seat and sheds, on whom the sacrificial stake
is reared,

174

On whom the Yajus-knowing priests recite their hymns
and chant their psalms,
And ministers are busied that Indra may drink the Soma
juice || 38

On whom the ancient Rishis, they who made the world,
sang forth the cows,
Seven worshippers, by session, with their fervent zeal
and sacrifice; || 39

May she, the Earth, assign to us the opulence for which
we yearn,
May Bhaga share and aid the task and Indra come to lead
the way. || 40

May she, the Earth, whereon men sing and dance with
varied shout and noise,
Whereon men meet in battle, and the war-cry and the
drum resound,
May she drive off our foemen, may Prithivī rid me of my
foes. || 41

On whom is food, barley and rice, to whom these Races
Five belong,
Homage to her, P arjanya's wife, to her whose marrow is
the rain! || 42

यस्याः पुरो देवकृताः क्षेत्रे यस्यां विकुर्वते ।
प्रजापतिः पृथिवीं विश्वगर्भामाशामाशां रयां नः कृणोतु ॥४३॥

निधिं बिभ्रती बहुधा गुहा वसु मणिं हिरण्यं पृथिवी दंदातु मे ।
वसूनि नो वसुदा रासमाना देवी दधातु सुमनस्यमाना ॥४४॥

जनं बिभ्रती बहुधा विवाचसं नानाधर्माणं पृथिवी यथौकसम् ।

Whose castles are the work of Gods, and men wage war upon her plain

The Lord of Life make Prithivī, who beareth all things in her womb, pleasant to us on every side! ‖ 43

May Earth the Goddess, she who bears her treasure stored up in many a place, gold, gems, and riches,

Giver of opulence, grant great possessions to us bestowing them with love and favour. ‖ 44

सहस्रं धारा द्रविणस्य मे दुहां ध्रुवेव धेनुरनपस्फुरन्ती ॥४५॥

यस्ते सर्पो वृश्चिकस्तृष्टदंशमा हेमन्तजब्धो भृमलो गुहा शये ।
क्रिमिर्जिन्वत्पृथिवि यद्यदेजति प्रावृषि तन्नः सर्पन्मोप सृपद्यच्छिवं तेन नो
मृड ॥४६॥

ये ते पन्थानो बहवो जनायना रथस्य वर्त्मानसश्च यातवे ।
यैः संचरन्त्युभये भद्रपापास्तं पन्थानं जयेमानमित्रमतस्करं यच्छिवं तेन
नो मृड ॥४७॥

मुल्वं बिभ्रती गुरुभृद्द्रपापस्य निधनं तितिन्नुः ।
वराहेण पृथिवी संविदाना सूकराय वि जिहीते मृगाय ॥४८॥

ये त आरण्याः पशवो मृगा वने हिताः सिंहा व्याघ्राः पुरुषादश्चरन्ति ।
उलं वृकं पृथिवि दुच्छूनामित ऋच्छीकां रक्षो अप बाधयास्मत् ॥४९॥

ये गन्धर्वा अप्सरसो ये चारायाः किमीदिनः ।
पिशाचान्त्सर्वा रक्षांसि तानुस्मद्धेमे यावय ॥५०॥

Earth, bearing folk of many a varied language with diverse
rites as suits their dwelling-places,

Pour, like a constant cow that never faileth, a thousand
streams of treasure to enrich me! || 45

Thy snake, thy sharply stinging scorpion, lying concealed,
bewildered, chilled with cold of winter,

The worm, O Prithivī, each thing that in the Rains revives
and stirs,

Creeping, forbear to creep on us! With all things gracious
bless thou us. || 46

177

Thy many ways on which the people travel, the road for car
and wain to journey over,

Thereon meet both the good and bad, that pathway may
we attain without a foe or robber.

With all things gracious bless thou us. || 47

Supporting both the foolish and the weighty she bears the
death both of the good and evil.

In friendly concord with the boar, Earth opens herself for
the wild swine that roams the forest. || 48

All sylvan beasts of thine that love the woodlands, man-
eaters, forest-haunting, lions, tigers,

Hyena, wolf, Misfortune, evil spirit, drive from us, chase
the demons to a distance. || 49

Gandharvas and Apsarases, Kimīdins, and malignant
spirits, Pisāchas áll, and Rākshasas, these keep thou, Earth!
afar from us. || 50

यां द्विपादः पक्षिणः संपतन्ति हंसाः सुपर्णाः शकुना वयांसि ।
यस्यां वातो मातरिश्वेर्यते रजांसि कृरवंश्चयावयंश्च वृक्षान् ।
वातस्य प्रवामुपवामनु वात्युर्चिः ॥५१॥

यस्यां कृष्णमरुणं च संहिते अहोरात्रे विहिते भूम्यामधि ।
वर्षेण भूमिः पृथिवी वृतावृता सा नो दधातु भद्रया प्रिये धामनिधामनि
॥५२॥

द्यौश्च म इदं पृथिवी चान्तरिक्षं च मे व्यचः ।

178

To whom the winged bipeds fly together, birds of each various kind, the swans, the eagles; On whom the Wind comes rushing, Mātarisvan, rousing the dust and causing trees to tremble, and flame pursues the blast hither and thither; || 51

Earth, upon whom are settled, joined together, the night and day, the dusky and the ruddy, Prithivī compassed by the rain about her, Happily may she stablish us in each delightful dwelling place. || 52

अग्निः सूर्य आपो मेधां विश्वे देवाश्च सं ददुः ॥५३॥

अहमस्मि सहमान उत्तरो नाम भूम्याम् ।
अभीषाडस्मि विश्वाषाडाशामाशां विषासहिः ॥५४॥

अदो यद्देवि प्रथमाना पुरस्ताद्देवैरुक्ता व्यसर्पो महित्वम् ।
आ त्वा सुभूतमविशत्तदानीमकल्पयथाः प्रदिशश्चतस्रः ॥५५॥

ये ग्रामा यदरण्यं याः सभा अधि भूम्याम् ।
ये संग्रामाः समितयस्तेषु चारु वदेम ते ॥५६॥

अश्व इव रजो दुधुवे वि तान्जनान्य आर्धियन्पृथिवीं यादजायत ।
मन्द्राग्रेत्वरी भुवनस्य गोपा वनस्पतीनां गृभिरोषधीनाम् ॥५७॥

यद्ददामि मधुमत्तद्ददामि यदीच्छे तद्दनन्ति मा ।
त्विषीमानस्मि जूतिमानवान्यान्हन्मि दोधतः ॥५८॥

शन्तिवा सुरभिः स्योना कीलालोध्नी पयस्वती ।
भूमिरधि ब्रवीतु मे पृथिवी पयसा सह ॥५९॥

179

Heaven, Earth, the realm of Middle Air have granted me this ample room,

Agni, Sun, Waters, all the Gods have joined to give me mental power. || 53

I am victorious, I am called the lord superior on earth,

Triumphant, all-o'erpowering the conqueror on every side || 54

There, when the Gods, O Goddess, named thee, spreading thy wide expanse as thou wast broadening eastward,

Then into thee passed many a charm and glory: thou madest for thyself the world's four regions. || 55

In hamlets and in woodland, and in all assemblages on earth,

In gatherings, meeting of the folk, we will speak glorious things of thee. || 56

As the horse scattereth the dust, the people who dwelt upon the land, at birth, she scattered,

Leader and head of all the world, delightful, the trees' protectress and the plants' upholder. || 57

Whate'er I say I speak with honey-sweetness, whatever I behold for that they love me.

Dazzling, impetuous am I: others who fiercely stir I slay. ||
58

Mild, gracious, sweetly odorous, milky, with nectar in her
breast,

May Earth, may Prithivī bestow her benison, with milk, on
me. || 59

यामन्वैच्छद्द्रविषा विश्वकर्मान्तरर्णवे रजसि प्रविष्टाम् ।
भुजिष्यं३ पात्रं निहितं गुहा यदाविर्भोगे अभवन्मातृमद्भः ॥६०॥

त्वमस्यावपनी जनानामदितिः कामदुघा पप्रथाना ।
यत्त ऊनं तत्त आ पूरयाति प्रजापतिः प्रथमजा ऋतस्य ॥६१॥

उपस्थास्ते अनमीवा अयक्ष्मा अस्मभ्यं सन्तु पृथिवि प्रसूताः ।
दीर्घं न आयुः प्रतिबुध्यमाना वयं तुभ्यं बलिहृतः स्याम ॥६२॥

Whom Visvakarman with oblation followed, when she was
set in mid-air's billowy ocean

A useful vessel, hid, when, for enjoyment, she was made
manifest to those with mothers. || 60

Thou art the vessel that containeth people, Aditi, granter of
the wish, far-spreading.

Prajāpati, the first-born Son of Order, supplieth thee with
whatsoe'er thou lackest. || 61

Let thy breasts free from sickness and Consumption be,
Prithivī, produced for our advantage.

181

Through long-extended life wakeful and watching still may we be thy tributary servants. || 62

भूमें मातुनिं धेहि मा भद्रया सुप्रतिष्ठितम् ।
संविदाना दिवा कवे श्रियां मा धेहि भूत्याम् ॥६३॥

O Earth, my Mother, set thou me happily in a place secure. Of one accord with Heaven, O Sage, set me in glory and in wealth. || 63

Atharva Veda 12.1-63 (trans. by Maurice Bloomfield, *Sacred Books of the East,* Vol. 42, 1897)

BOOK XII

HYMN I

A hymn of prayer and praise to Prithivī or deified Earth

1Truth, high and potent Law, the Consecrating Rite, Fervour,   Brahma, and Sacrifice uphold the Earth.
  May she, the Queen of all that is and is to be, may Prithivī
    make ample space and room for us.
2Not over awded by the crowd of Manu's sons, she who hath many heights and floods and level plains;
  She who bears plants endowed with many varied powers,

may Prithivī for us spread wide and favour us.

3In whom the sea, and Sindhu, and the waters, in whom our food and corn-lands had their being,

In whom this all that breathes and moves is active, this Earth assign us foremost rank and station!

4She who is Lady of the earth's four regions, in whom our food and corn-lands had their being,

Nurse in each place of breathing, moving creatures, this Earth vouchsafe us kine with milk that fails not!

5On whom the men of old before us battled, on whom the Gods attacked the hostile demons,

The varied home of bird, and kine and horses, this Prithivī vouchsafe us luck and splendour!

6Firm standing-place, all-bearing, store of treasures, gold-breasted, harbourer of all that moveth.

May Earth who bears Agni Vaisvānara, Consort of mighty Indra, give us great possessions

7May Earth, may Prithivī, always protected with ceaseless care by Gods who never slumber,

May she pour out for us delicious nectar, may she bedew us with a flood of splendour.

8She who at first was water in the ocean, whom with their wond rous powers the sages followed,

May she whose heart is in the highest heaven, compassed about with truth, and everlasting,

May she, this Earth, bestow upon us lustre, and grant us power in loftiest dominion.

9On whom the running universal waters flow day and night with never-ceasing motion,

May she with many streams pour milk to feed us, may she bedew us with a flood of splendour.

10She whom the Asvins measured out, o'er whom the foot of Vishnu strode,

Whom Indra, Lord of Power and Might, freed from all foemen for himself,

May Earth pour out her milk for us, a mother unto me her son.

11O Prithivī, auspicious be thy woodlands, auspicious be thy hills and snow-clad mountains.

Unslain, unwounded, unsubdued, I have set foot upon the Earth, On earth brown, black, ruddy and every-coloured, on the firm earth that Indra guards from danger.

12O Prithivī, thy centre and thy navel, all forces that have issued from thy body

Set us amid those forces; breathe upon us. I am the son of

Earth, Earth is my Mother. Parjanya is my Sire; may he promote me.

43Earth on whose surface they enclose the altar, and all-performers spin the thread of worship;

In whom the stakes of sacrifice, resplendent, are fixed and raised on high before the oblation, may she, this Earth, prospering, make us prosper.

14The man who hates us, Earth! who fights against us, who threaten us with thought or deadly weapon, make him our thrall as thou hast done aforetime.

15Produced from thee, on thee move mortal creatures: thou bearest them, both quadruped and biped.

Thine, Prithivī, are these Five human Races, for whom, though mortal, Sūrya as he rises spreads with his rays the light that is immortal.

16In concert may these creatures yield us blessings. With honey of discourse, O Earth, endow me.

17Kind, ever gracious be the Earth we tread on, the firm Earth, Prithivī, borne up by Order, mother of plants and herbs, the all-producer.

18A vast abode hast thou become, the Mighty. Great stress is on thee, press and agitation, but with unceasing care great Indra guards thee.

So make us shine, O Earth, us with the splendour of gold. Let no man look on us with hatred.

19Agni is in the earth, in plants; the waters hold Agni in them, in the stones is Agni.

Agni abideth deep in men: Agnis abide in cows and steeds.

20Agni gives shine and heat in heaven: the spacious air is his, the God's Lover of fatness, bearer of oblation, men enkindle him.

21Dark-kneed, invested with a fiery mantle, Prithivī sharpen me and give me splendour!

22On earth they offer sacrifice and dressed oblation to the Gods.

Men, mortals, live upon the earth by food in their accustomed way.

May that Earth grant us breath and vital power. Prithivī give me life of long duration!

23Scent that hath risen from thee, O Earth, the fragrance which growing herbs and plants and waters carry,

Shared by Apsarases, shared by Gandharvas therewith make thou me sweet: let no man hate me.

24Thy scent which entered and possessed the lotus, the scent which they prepared at Sūryā's bridal,

Scent which Immortals Earth! of old collected, therewith make thou me sweet: let no man hate me.

25Thy scent in women and in men, the luck and light that is in. males,

That is in heroes and in steeds in sylvan beasts and elephants, The splendid energy of maids, therewith do thou unite us,.Earth! Let no man look on us with hate.

26Rock earth, and stone, and dust, this Earth is held together   firmly bound.

To this gold-breasted Prithivī mine adoration have I paid.

27Hither we call the firmly held, the all-supporting Prithivī,

On whom the trees, lords of the wood, stand evermore immovable.

28Sitting at ease or rising up, standing or going on our way.

With our right foot and with our left we will not reel upon the earth.

29I speak to Prithivī the purifier, to patient Earth who groweth strong through Brahma.

O Earth, may we recline on thee who bearest strength, increase, portioned share of food, and fatness.

30Purified for our bodies flow the waters: we bring distress on him who would attack us.

I cleanse myself, O Earth, with that which cleanseth.

31Earth, be thine eastern and thy northern regions, those lying southward and those lying westward.

Propitious unto me in all my movements. Long as I tread the ground let me not stumble.

32Drive us not from the west or east, drive us not from the north or south,

Be gracious unto us, O Earth: let not the robbers find us; keep the deadly weapon far away.

33Long as, on thee, I look around, possessing Sūrya as a friend,

So long, through each succeeding year, let not my power of vision fail.

34When, as I lie, O Earth, I turn upon my right side and my left,

When stretched at all our length we lay our ribs on thee who meetest us.

Do us no injury there, O Earth who furnishest a bed for all.

35Let what I dig from thee, O Earth, rapidly spring and grow again.

O Purifier, let me not pierce through thy vitals or thy heart

36Earth, may thy summer, and thy rains, and autumn, thy winter, and thy dewy frosts, and spring-time.

May thy years, Prithivī! and ordered seasons, and day and
  night pour out for us abundance.
37The purifier, shrinking from the Serpent, she who held
fires that lie within the waters,
  Who gives as prey the God-blaspheming Dasyus, Earth
choosing Indra for her Lord, not Vritra, hath clung to
Sakra, to the Strong and Mighty.
38Base of the seat and sheds, on whom the sacrificial stake
is reared,
  On whom the Yajus-knowing priests recite their hymns
and chant their psalms,
  And ministers are busied that Indra may drink the Soma
juice;
39On whom the ancient Rishis, they who made the world,
sang forth the cows,
  Seven worshippers, by session, with their fervent zeal and
    sacrifice;
40May she, the Earth, assign to us the opulence for which
we yearn,
  May Bhaga share and aid the task and Indra come to lead
the way.
41May she, the Earth, whereon men sing and dance with
varied shout and noise,

Whereon men meet in battle, and the war-cry and the drum resound,

May she drive off our foemen, may Prithivī rid me of my foes.

42On whom is food, barley and rice, to whom these Races Five belong,

Homage to her, P arjanya's wife, to her whose marrow is the rain!

43Whose castles are the work of Gods, and men wage war upon her plain

The Lord of Life make Prithivī, who beareth all things in her womb, pleasant to us on every side!

44May Earth the Goddess, she who bears her treasure stored up in many a place, gold, gems, and riches,

Giver of opulence, grant great possessions to us bestowing them with love and favour.

45Earth, bearing folk of many a varied language with divers rites as suits their dwelling-places,

Pour, like a constant cow that never faileth, a thousand streams of treasure to enrich me!

46Thy snake, thy sharply stinging scorpion, lying concealed, bewildered, chilled with cold of winter,

The worm, O Prithivī, each thing that in the Rains revives

and stirs,

Creeping, forbear to creep on us! With all things gracious bless thou us.

47Thy many ways on which the people travel, the road for car and wain to journey over,

Thereon meet both the good and bad, that pathway may we attain without a foe or robber. With all things gracious bless thou us.

48Supporting both the foolish and the weighty she bears the death both of the good and evil.

In friendly concord with the boar, Earth opens herself for the wild swine that roams the forest.

49All sylvan beasts of thine that love the woodlands, man-eaters,.forest-haunting, lions, tigers,

Hyena, wolf, Misfortune, evil spirit, drive from us, chase the demons to a distance.

50Gandharvas and Apsarases, Kimīdins, and malignant sprites, Pisāchas all, and Rākshasas, these keep thou, Earth! afar from us.

51To whom the winged bipeds fly together, birds of each various kind, the swans, the eagles;

On whom the Wind comes rushing, Mātarisvan, rousing the dust and causing trees to tremble, and flame pursues the blast. hither and thither;

52Earth, upon whom are settled, joined together, the night and day, the dusky and the ruddy, Prithivī compassed by the rain about her,

Happily may she stablish us in each delightful dwelling place.

53Heaven, Earth, the realm of Middle Air have granted me this ample room,

Agni, Sun, Waters, all the Gods have joined to give me mental power.

54I am victorious, I am called the lord superior on earth,

Triumphant, all-o'erpowering the conqueror on every side

55There, when the Gods, O Goddess, named thee, spreading thy wide expanse as thou wast broadening eastward,

Then into thee passed many a charm and glory: thou madest for thyself the world's four regions.

56In hamlets and in woodland, and in all assemblages on earth, In gatherings, meeting of the folk, we will speak glorious things of thee.

57As the horse scattereth the dust, the people who dwelt upon the land, at birth, she scattered,

Leader and head of all the world, delightful, the trees'

protectress and the plants' upholder.

58Whate'er I say I speak with honey-sweetness, whatever I behold for that they love me.

Dazzling, impetuous am I: others who fiercely stir I slay.

59Mild, gracious, sweetly odorous, milky, with nectar in her breast,

May Earth, may Prithivī bestow her benison, with milk, on me.

60Whom Visvakarman with oblation followed, when she was set in mid-air's billowy ocean

A useful vessel, hid, when, for enjoyment, she was made manifest to those with mothers.

61Thou art the vessel that containeth people, Aditi, granter of the wish, far-spreading. Prajāpati, the first-born Son of Order, supplieth thee with what- soe'er thou lackest.

62Let thy breasts, frec from sickness and Consumption, be.

Prithivī, produced for our advantage.

Through long-extended life wakeful and watching still may we be thy tributary servants.

63O Earth, my Mother, set thou me happily in a place secure.

Of one accord with Heaven, O Sage, set me in glory and in wealth.[68]

The absence of discrimination, provisions to check abuse of power and enjoining the state to promote the individual's and samajam's activities for the attainment of purushartha [achieving the goals of life -- of dharma (righteous conduct), of artha (economic well-being) and of kāma (mental well-being)] are the key facets of rajadharma. Such a rajadharma is beyond secular and is a sacred trust to be administered with diligence and commitment.

Such a rājadharma is exemplified by ramarajyam which is evoked by many rulers of Bharatam in many parts of the nation in their references to Sri Ramachandra as the ideal ruler whose example the rulers hoped to emulate in rendering social justice and in regulating the affairs of the state. Rāmarājyam is a dharma polity, governed by a dharma constitution. This is the reason why Valmiki refers to Rama in eloquent terms: Rāmo vigrahavān dharmah. (Rama is the very embodiment of dharma).

The supremacy of dharma is emphasized in Brhadaranyakopanisad:

> tadetat kṣatrasya kṣatram yaddharmah
>
> tasmāddharmātparam nāsti
>
> atho abalīyān balīyāmsamāśamsate dharmeṇa

yatha rājā evam

The law (Dharma) is the king of kings. No one is superior to Dharma. The Dharma aided by the power of the king enables the weak to prevail over the strong.

This is further emphasised in Karṇa Parva (ch. 69, verse 58):

dhāraṇād dharma ity āhurdharmo dhārayate prajāh

yat syād dhāraṇasamyuktam sa dharma iti niścayah

Dharma sustains the society; Dharma maintains the social order; Dharma ensures well-being and progress of humanity; Dharms is surely that which fulfils these objectives.

The two great epics Ramayana and Mahabharata and the Bhagavata Purana explain dharma in action, the application of the 'ordering principles' in specific real-life situations, in moments of creative tension such as when a proponent like Arjuna had to decide to fight against his own kith and kin, members of his own kula. This moment of decision results in the delineation of the Dharmakshetra (the domain of dharma) in that Song Celestial, Bhagavad Gita. An enduring metaphor of the Bhagavatam is samudra manthanam: deva and asura apparently in conflict work

together to harness the resources of the ocean by churning
the ocean together.

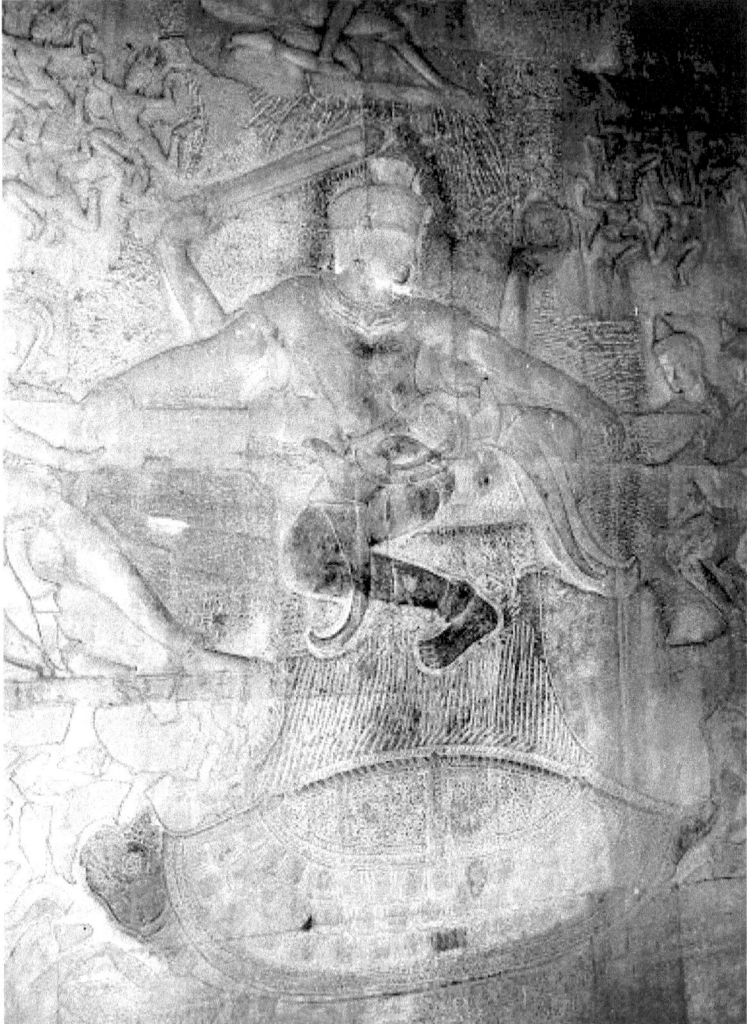

The bas-relief from Angkor Wat, Cambodia, shows
Samudra manthan-Vishnu in the centre, his turtle Avatar
Kurma below, asuras and devas to left and right.

This is an economic metaphor *par excellence* from Bhāgavata Purāṇa attesting to co-operative endeavours to acquire wealth by churning the oceans.

This togetherness to achieve artha and kaama is a dharmic cooperative endeavour, an example of a samajam in harmony, pulling together for a common purpose – that purpose is loka hitam, 'well-being of loka'. Loka hitam is the touchstone which determines the dharmic nature of positive action. Just as satyam is truth that is pleasing, dharma is action which is loka-hitaaya 'for the well-being of the society'. How should such action be performed or such responsibility be discharged? Governed by ethical conduct, a social ethic which respects the responsibilities being discharged by everyone in society.

Dharma is sacred because it is the divine ordering principle. Dharma is the principle which recognizes the way things are or the nature of things or phenomena. In Thai language, the compound dharmacarth (dharma carati) means 'nature'. Hence, the compound sva-dharma in the evolution of sanātana dharma (Eternal global ethic) in Bhāratam, means 'law and responsibility, according to one's nature'.

Rigveda notes that ṛtam 'occurrence of phenomena' or 'order' is dharma. Atharva Veda notes: Prithivīm dharmaṇādhṛtam 'the world is upheld by dharma'. Sanātana Dharma in bhāratiya metaphysics (elaborated further in Buddha, Jaina, Khalsa pantha thought) is not a moral connotation. It is an inexorable organizing, creative principle which operates on the plane of the aatman and the cosmos.

Sanātana dharma is thus beyond a law regulating an individual's action. It is the very expression of the divine. Such adherence to the divine principle is the purusharta, the purpose of life.

Let us see how an Egyptian islamist understood dharma: "It [dharma] is, so to speak, the essential nature of a being, comprising the sum of its particular qualities or characteristics, and determining, by virtue of the tendencies or dispositions it implies, the manner in which this being will conduct itself, either in a general way or in relation to each particular circumstance. The same idea may be applied, not only to a single being, but also to an organized collectivity, to a species, to all the beings included in a cosmic cycle or state of existence, or even to the whole order of the Universe; it then, at one level or another, signifies conformity with the essential nature of beings..."[69]

Bhishma explained to Yudhishthira: "It is very difficult to define the dharma. Dharma was explained as that which helps the elevation of the human. This is the reason, this that assures well-being is assuredly dharma. The learned rishis declared: this that supports is dharma."

Like satyam, dharma was explained with reference to the beneficial effect it generates: well-being and progress of humanity. "Dharma is this that supports and that assures the progress and the well-being of all in this world and the eternal happiness in the other world. Dharma is promulgated in the form of orders (positive and negative: Vidhi and Nishedha)." This was the elucidaton of Madhvacharya in his commentary on Parasarasmruti. This rendering of the semantics of dharma explains why dharma covered all aspects of life for the well-being of the individual and also the *samājam* (society).

The Karna Parva, Ch. 59, verse 58, praises the dharma in the following terms:

The Dharma supports the corporation, The Dharma maintains the social order, The Dharma assures well-being and the progress of humanity, The Dharma is certainly this that fills these objectives."

Jaimini, the author of the famous Purvamimamsa and uthara Mimamsa, explains that:

Dharma-dhamma is this that is indicated in the Vedas as driving to the biggest good.

"Though the country and the people may be divided into different states (provinces) for convenience of administration, the country is one integral whole, its people a single people living under a single imperium derived from a single source." -- Dr. B.R.Ambedkar, Chairman, Drafting Committee of the Constitution of India

Justice Madan Mohan Punchhi, Former Chief Justice of India was appointed in April 2007, to head a Commission on Centre-State Relations . The Commission's Report in 7 volumes was presented to Govt. of India on 31 March 2010. An earlier Commission on Centre-State (Province) Relations (referred to as the Sarkaria Commission after the name of its Chairman Mr. Justice R.S. Sarkaria) in its report submitted in 1988 observed:- "Decentralisation of real power to local institutions would help defuse the threat of centrifugal forces, increase popular involvement all along the line, broaden the base of our democratic polity, promote administrative efficiency and improve the health

and stability of inter-governmental relations …………
Unfortunately, there was not only inadequate territorial and
functional decentralization in India when the country
became independent, but there has also been a pervasive
trend towards greater centralization of powers over the
years, inter alia, due to the pressure of powerful socio-
economic forces."[70]

Recognizing this democratic deficit, the Constitution was
amended in 1992 (73rd and 74th Constitution Amendment
Acts) to introduce a third tier system of governance at the
level of Panchayats and Municipalities.

The question posed to the Punchhi Commission was: 'Are
the existing arrangements governing Centre-State
(Province) relations – legislative, executive and financial –
envisaged in the Constitution as they have evolved over the
years, working in a manner that can meet the aspirations of
the Indian society as also the requirements of an
increasingly globalizing world? If not, what are the
impediments and how can they be remedied without
violating the basic structure of the Constitution?'

The Punchhi commission notes: "The dictum of 'basic
structure' of the Constitution propounded by the Supreme

Court in the celebrated *Keshavananda Bharati* case also tied the hands of the Centre in important ways. The effect, *inter alia*, was that while the States (Provinces) felt handicapped in pursuing development programmes of their own for lack of adequate funds, the Centre found itself hamstrung even when there was serious breakdown in law and order in some areas." (Vol. 1, p. xxi)

Making over 200 recommendations, the Punchhi Commission also recommended amendment of Articles 355 and 356 to enable Central rule of trouble-torn areas, an internal security structure on the lines of the US Homeland Security department, making National Integration Council meaningful by making NIC meet at least once a year, and amending the Communal Violence Bill to allow deployment of Central forces without the state's (province's) consent for a short period, removal of a Governor through impeachment by the State (Province) assembly and providing for a say to the state (Province) Chief Minister in the appointment of governor, giving a right to the Governor to sanction prosecution of a minister against the advice of the council of ministers.

Overall, the recommendations of the two Commissions -- Sarkaria Commission and Punchhi Commission – have been disappointing skirting the main issue of resolving the developmental imperative of the ratram with the security imperative of the Rāṣṭram.

Both the Commissions and the standing Finance Commissions which have been appointed every five years, have missed the wood for the trees, by suggesting tinkering with the system by looking at the instruments of state as instruments of violence.

These Commissions have failed to recognize the serious threats faced by the Rāṣṭram on the key issues of integrity and security caused by 1) the threats of destroying the polity by criminalization and corrupt practices; and 2) the national security threats from external and internal sources of fomenting communal tensions, by Naxalite or Maoist insurgencies and hostile neighbours seeking lebensraum.

The colonial loot of unprecedented dimensions have been rivaled by the post-colonial loot by stashing away black money in tax havens abroad. (One estimate given by Director, CBI reckons this at US Dollars 500 billion, that is, Rs. 20 lakh crores). Effective remedial measures have not been suggested to undo the devastation caused to national integration efforts by the formation of Pakistan and by not commending steps to implement Article 44 of the Constitution of India which calls for a Uniform Civil Code. Article 44 is merely the first step in achieving a sense of identity among all citizens of India that they owe allegiance to the Rāṣṭram, saying no to sectarian ideologies and false denominations of secularism.

While all men are created equal, traditions of India, that is Bharat, hold that dharma-dhamma has endowed us with certain unalienable responsibilities for abhyudayam and nihshreyas (social welfare and individual unity of the atman with paramatman). The Rāṣṭram is a dharma-dhamma saapeksha Rāṣṭram. This inalienable dictum, this dharma-dhamma, this foundation of the Rāṣṭram which cannot be surrendered, sold or transferred for any ideology, should get enshrined in the Preamble to the Constitution by declaring a dharma-dhamma saapeksha Rāṣṭram. This dharma-dhamma declaration should precede any attempt to restate the structural features of the state.

If this Constitutional Amendment is beyond the powers of the Parliament pace Keshavananda Bharati case, let there be a new Constituent Assembly to redraw the dharma constitution for the Rāṣṭram. The absurd definition of secularism gets exemplified by devious attempts made to translate 'secular' in the Preamble as 'dharma nirapekshata' in Hindi official version of the Constitution kept in Rashtrapati Bhavan. Luckily, this bizarre translation was NOT approved and the word 'secular' was translated into Hindi as: 'pantha nirapekshata', that is, neutrality as to individual religious path preferences.

How should a dharma sāpekṣa Rāṣṭram be structured? Rāṣṭram is the path which enlightens. The supreme divinity is rastrii, the divine force which defines all dharmas in all walks of life and all facets of existence in a sustainable global order for wealth creation, equitable distribution and use. Such a Rāṣṭram calls for a United States along the Indian Ocean Rim to create an Indian Ocean Community remembering that the largest Vishnu mandiram of the globe is in Angkor Wat, Cambodia. Such a federation of about 59 states along the Indian Indian Ocean Rim will be an economic powerhouse for abhyudayam of over 2 billion people. This organization can undo the raves of the colonial regimes which left many of these states in an impoverished state.

Such a federating union has to federate local communities, recognized as Panchayats or Municipalities or Corporations in the Indian state and comparable formations in other states of the Indian Ocean Rim.

The imperative of empowering local communities, janapadas will be consonant with the traditional forms which had evolved over millennia for involving the people of the janapadas in socio-economic activities. A good example is provided by the Uttaramerur inscription of the 12th century which described the formation of village councils after due democratic elections and after due process of selecting council members of exemplary rectitude, from within the community. Such localization of developmental activity (abhyudayam) will mean the transfer of power directly to the people. This transfer has to become meaningful by an automatic transfer of central finances directly to the panchayat raj institutions for projects such as local, small-scale industries, maintenance of roads, building and maintenance of schools, primary health-care centers and other civic responsibilities of the panchayat. The Panchayat will also have to be empowered to monitor the functioning of large industries within the geographical domain of the Panchayat, even if it means the control of, say, a nuclear power station. The present structure of central-state (province) division of responsibilities by State (Province), Central and Concurrent Lists has to be radically revamped to entrust responsibilities to the third tier, the Panchayat.

Peoples' Parliament

Inter-state transactions of trade, defense and foreign affairs can be the responsibility of the Centre. Providing for enabling legislative framework can be the responsibility of the state. The real executive has to be the Janapada, the Panchayat. This structural formation for a Rāṣṭram is a feasible proposition which can build upon the types of structures which have been proven to work effectively, for example, in Peoples' Republic of China. Decentralize for development and integrity of the state, centralize for security of the state from trans-border threats such as those from terrorism or religious conversion missions. A Peoples' Parliament can be brought into being to provide for an ideological umbrella to the Parliamentary institutions such as the Lok Sabha or Rajya Sabha in India. The Peoples' Parliament should be composed as a Constituent Assembly .

In India, there are 640 districts. Each district should elect four representatives from among the Panchayati Raj institutions to function as members of the Peoples' Parliament which is the Constituent Assembly. This Assembly should meet at least once a year to oversee the discharge of legislative functions entrusted to the Provinces and the Panchayats Raj institutions. The Peoples' Parliament should also define the Centre-Province-Panchayati Raj institutional responsibilities using three lists: Central List, Province List, Panchayat List. These Lists should be a total revamp of the existing Union, State and Concurrent Lists defining the responsibilities of the structural components of the India polity.

The structure of the Rāṣṭram as a trans-national structure, can be regulated with the following broad allocation of responsibilities, as lists, to the three constituent institutions: Constituent Assembly, State Parliament, Panchayat Administration.

Rāṣṭram list to include: Inter-state commerce and inter-state development projects such as Trans-Asian Highway, Trans-Asian Railway, Implementation of the Law of the Sea by extending territorial waters to 200 nautical miles from the base, Interpol.

State list to include: defence, atomic energy, foreign affairs, citizenship, transport, communication, currency..

Panchayat list to include: local government, education, police, justice, agriculture, commerce, banking, insurance, control of industries, development of mines, mineral and oil resources, elections, civil code, public health and sanitation, agriculture, animal husbandry, water supplies and irrigation, land rights, forests, fisheries.

Five dimensional economic model of Subramanian Swamy

India today leads the world in the supply pool of youth, i.e., persons in the age group of 15 to 35 years, and this lead will last for another forty years. This generation is most fertile milieu for promoting knowledge, innovation, and research. It is the prime work force that saves for the future, the corpus for pension funding of the old. We should therefore not squander this "natural vital resource".

Thus, India has now become, by unintended consequences, gifted with a young population. If we educate this youth to develop cognitive intelligence [CQ] to become original thinkers, imbibe emotional intelligence [EQ] to have team spirit and rational risk-taking attitude, inculcate moral intelligence [MQ] to blend personal ambition with national goals, cultivate social intelligence [SOI] to defend civic rights of the weak, gender equality, and the courage to fight injustice and nurture spiritual intelligence [SI] to innovate the transformative power of vision and intention to access the vast energy the pervades the cosmos to innovate and out of box research, then we can develop a superior species of human being, an Indian youth who can be relied on to contribute to make India a global power within two decades. Computers my have high CQ because they are programmed to understand the rules, and follow them without making mistakes. Many mammals have high EQ. Only humans know to ask why, and can work with re-shaping boundaries instead of just within boundaries. Human can innovate, not animals.

Many intelligences listed are comparable to the postulate of Mahavira, the 24th Tirthankara who propounded *anekānta*, the philosophy of non-absolutism. Anekānta postulates that assessment of anything should be relative to substance, space, time and *bhāva* (state of the *ātman)*. Anekānta thus rejects absolutism. Unlike laissez-faire which postulates absolute freedom to acquire wealth, unlike the capitalist manifesto which points to the inexorable march of capitalist history, Anekānta postulates non-absolutism and places every material phenomenon in a relativist framework.

The nation must therefore structure a national policy for the youth of India so that in every young Indian the five dimensional concept of intelligence, viz., cognitive emotional, moral, social and spiritual manifests in his character. Only then, our demographic dividend will not be wasted. These five dimensions of intelligence constitute the ability of a person to live a productive life and for national good. Hence, a policy for India's youth has to be structured within the implied parameters of these five dimensions.

True happiness is possible, according to Sanātana Dharma, only if material progress that is attained is moderated and harmonized by spiritual values. This is the Hindutva [Hinduness] principle of economic development and it is this core concept that is becoming widely acceptable faced with the consequences of greed and envy that is fueling the current globalization. Thus, the choice of objectives, priorities, strategy and financial architecture, the four pillars of the nation's policy-making for economic development, have to be defined in accordance with the Hindu concepts.

Deendayal Upadhyaya proposed self-reliance (swadeshi) and decentralization (vikendrikaran) as two pillars of economic policy to replace the capitalist-communist models premised on 1) fierce competition of selfih people or 2) people as feeble cogs requiring direction and rigid rules of dictatorship. The consequences of the models: 1) Selfishness bred greed. 2) Class struggle was anti-human. First, objective function. The alternative model avoids these consequences of 1) maximum profit in production theory and 2) maximum utility in consumer behavior. The alternative objectives will be: 1) minimum cost of production subject to a lower bound for production and 2) minimum expenditure subject to a lower bound for the level of utility to be attained. Trusteeship and philanthropy can become integral parts of social responsibility of every productive enterprise in śreṇi dharma – socially responsible corporate is the śreṇi .

Second, that while individual choices are transitive, collective majority determined choice is not necessarily transitive. Hence collective choice would require conflict resolution and game theory to ensure transitivity. This is the Hindutva principle of harmonization.

Third, that innovation would not be cognitive intelligence driven but by a collective determination of six intelligences—cognitive, emotional, social, moral, spiritual and environmental.

Postulates which have stirred the soulforce (chiti) – the unity of culture as the basis of homogeneity-- of a society:

Postulate 1. Economy is a sub-system of society

Postulate 2. Plurality and diversity have to be harmonized

Postulate 3. Negative correlation between State's coercive power and dharma

Postulate 4. A society has to realize its identity (chiti or soulforce)

Postulate 5. Social ownership of property can be harmonized with incentives to save and to produce

Postulte 5. Society led by innovation, optimum use of resources, decentralization

Postulate 6. Cognitive, emotional, social, moral, and spiritual intelligences

Decentralised polity can achieve better harmonization of or consensus on choices and preferences than a centralized decision making process.

Social capital model of Vaidyanathan

"Persons' actions are shaped, redirected, constrained by the social context; norms, interpersonal trust, social networks, and social organization are important in the functioning not only of the society but also of the economy."

Thus, one definition of social capital as: "....the rules, norms, obligations, reciprocity and trust embedded in social relations, social structures and society's institutional arrangements which enable members to achieve their individual and community objectives."

However defined, social capital is an economic good which affects economic performance. Economic rationality as a postulate finds varied expressions across nations, cultures and across stages of economic performance.

Five mechanisms describe how social capital affects outcomes . They are:

- Improve society's ability to monitor the performance of government, either because government officials are more embedded in the social network or because monitoring the public provision of services is a public good:

- Increase possibilities for co-operative action in solving problems with a local common property element;

- Facilitate the diffusion of innovations by increasing inter-linkages among individuals;

- Reduce information imperfections and expand the range of enforcement mechanisms, thereby increasing transactions in output, credit, land and labour markets;

- Increase informal insurance (or informal safety nets) between households, thereby allowing households to pursue higher returns, but more risky, activities and production techniques.

Some view trust as a feature of social organizations constituting social capital. Some view social networks as contributing to social capital. Some see social capitalism as the "common kernel" of the European welfare state and a "middle way" between socialist collectivism and neo-liberal individualism.

Vaidyanathan calls Indian economy a partnership/ proprietorship economy of 41.83 million enterprises (50% of which are owned by SC/ST/OBC; (Economic Census 2005). He contrasted Indian economy with USA where cororate sector accounts for more than 75% of the GDP (2010).

"A nation can be maintained only if between the state and the individual there is interposed a whole series of secondary groups near enough to the individuals to attract them strongly in their sphere of action and drag them, in this way, into the general torrent of social life... Occupational groups are suited to fill this role, and that is their identity... community orientation creates trust among the members of the society." This observation is endorsed by Fukuyama as: "the ability to associate depends, in turn on the degree to which communities share norms and values and are able to subordinate individual interests to those of larger groups. Out of such shared values comes trust and trust as we will see has a large and measurable economic Value and trust results in social capital."

In the Gross Domestic Savings Rs. 2,207,423 crores of 2010 (33.7% of GDP in 2010), household savings account for 23.5% of GDP. Foreign investment flows were Rs. 329,815 crores in 2010 (15% of GDP)

He notes that services sector principally driven by domestic savings, accounts for nearly 63% of Indian economy. More than 75% of activities of this sector are in construction, trade, hotels and restaurants, non-railway transport and real estate, business services.

Table. Share of Gross Domestic Product (%)

Category	2004-2005	2009-2010
Agriculture and forestry, fishing	19.0	17.8
Mining, manufacturing, electricity	20.3	18.8
Services	60.7	63.4
Total	100	100

Notes: 1. At constant 2004-2005 prices 2. We have included construction as part of services[71]

Economic census of 2005 by Central Statistical Organization (CSO) indicated a total of 41.83 million enterprises in different economic activities other than crop production and plantation. 90% of these enterprises were self-financing,and did not depend upon financial institutions. About 50.54% of these enterprises were owned by SC/ST/OBC. In the manufacturing sector, approximately In 1999, 350 small scale industrial clusters and about 2000 rural and artisan-based clusters contributed to 60% of manufacturing exports and 40% of employment in the manufacturing industry. Such clusters tend to be relation-ship- or caste-based indicative of social capital generation. Vaidyanathan concludes: "The economic development has taken place in the "India Uninc" or the partnership/proprietorship activities financed by domestic savings and facilitated by clusters and caste/community networks. Actually caste has been a major social capital in our growth process..."

Household economics

-- Rebuilding economic theory founded on the household

Economics is a term derived from ancient Greek οἰκονομία (*oikonomia*, "management of a household, administration") from οἶκος (*oikos*, "house") + νόμος (*nomos*, "custom" or "law"), hence "rules of the house(hold)".

A more comprehensive term to denote economic transactions or exchanges among households is artha. The term originally meant 'aim, purpose' in Rgveda and Manu, later expanded to mean "motive, meaning, notion, wealth, economy or gain".

Artha is a purpose of life together with *dharma, kāma* and *mokṣa*. Artha is directly related to the stage of life as a householder, when he or she has to acquire wealth for the benefit of present and future generations. In the āśrama system based on progressive developmental stages of life, human activity is divided into the stages of *Brahmacharya* (student life), *Grihastha* (household life), *Vānaprastha* (retired life), *Sannyasa* (renounced life). The stage of household life is devoted to acquisition of artha, wealth – the principal economic activity. Thus artha refers to material prosperity or wealth, which in Hindu thought is one of the four goals of life or *purushārtha* (purposes of life as human, *puruṣa*). In terms of social organization, varṇāśrama refers to four Hindu social orders, all participating in the acquisition of wealth: Brahmin (priests), Kshatriyas (warriors), Vaiśyas (traders) śudras (workmen). In China, the omparable Fengjian social structure (c. 1046–256 BCE) had *shi* (gentry scholars), the *nong* (peasant farmers), the *gong* (artisans and craftsmen), and the *shang* (merchants and traders). A comparable organization in Proto-Indo-European society was three classes: priests, warriors and commoners (traders or tradesmen).[72]

Economics as a social science should be concerned with artha and the social order generating artha, wealth, has to be consistent with the global ethical order called dharma, the upholding principle (*dhr̥*, 'to uphold, support') of the world.

Economics as a social science has gone far beyond the management rules for a household and has expanded its domain to dominate and control the society itself.

Political economy is an extension of the term to denote the dominant role played by the state dictating how private lives are lived.

The expanded role of economics involves state as a dominant player, resulting from the instrument of money, which is regulated as a state fiction to fcilitate exchange transactions between and among households.
The expanded role is exemplified by Adam Smith's 'An enquiry into the nature and causes of the wealth of nations' (1776). This work has led to the use of the term 'wealth' as a central concept in economics.

Are markets and state power an efficient and effective consortium which can be allowed to dictate how one should live one's life in a household?

Though economics deals with 'scarcity' of demand to match 'abundant' wants, the emphasis on wealth is significant because wealth is defined as 'abundance of valuable resources or material possessions'. An alternative term used is 'capital' as sums of money or assets put to productive use. As a factor of production (distinct from land or labor or technology/ entrepreneurship as other factors), economics of capitalism deals with capital as a proxy for wealth. Communism restricts the definition of capital[73] to the process of its circulation creating wealth, to realize a profit

In many societies, corporations operating through markets control only a small percentage of economic activities in the society. In India, for example, the 'unincorporated' sector, that is productive enterprises operating outside the markets account for the major share of the Gross Domestic Product (GDP).

Today, markets are controlled by corporations co-opted [74] with state power. In reality, individuals are not free actors in the marketplace. The dominant players in the markets are states and corporations. Individuals dance to the tunes of speculators rife in the markets and of states which dictate the 'value' of money through central banking institutions and fiscal policies.

'Market fundamentalism' has engulfed the globe and has sucked in its insatiable appetite, even socialist and communist structures represented by polities such as the Russian Federation or the Peoples' Republic of China. The fall of the Berlin wall in November 1989 is a history marker for the march of global capitalism.

Global capitalism is principally concerned with manipulation of ownership, ignoring the imperative of or paying lip-service to augmenting wealth of nations.

Market fundamentalism is a term used not only by the billionaire George Soros but also by adherents of interventionist/protectionist positions and mixed economies, apart from economists[75]. Adam Smith noted that markets function best when the "unseen hand" gets minimal interference from government. The underlying fundamentalist postulate was that markets tend towards a natural equilibrium when market participants pusue their own financial interests.

Market fundamentalism evolved from this axiom which was applied to limited liability corporations, despite Adam Smith's abhorrence of abuses by transnational corporations such as the East India Company in India and the American colonies. What Smith propounded was encouragement of small, local players, kept free from the influence of

powerful corporations and without governmental
interference.

Corporations were entitled to the same property rights as
individuals but were exempted from liability that
individuals do not have. This created a political economy
with basic inequality of rights. (Bidstrup, Scott. 2002, Free
Market Fundamentalism: Friedman, Pinochet and the
"Chilean Miracle",)

It should be noted that corporation is an ancient Indian
form of business organization. The examination by
Vikramaditya Khanna[76] on the history and development of
Indian corporate form reveals: "that business people on the
Indian subcontinent utilized the corporate form from a very
early period. The corporate form (e.g., the śreṇi) was being
used in India from at least 800 B.C., and perhaps even
earlier, and was in more or less continuous use since then
until the advent of the Islamic invasions around 1000 A.D.
This provides evidence for the use of the corporate form
centuries before the earliest Roman proto-corporations. In
fact, the use of the śreṇi in Ancient India was widespread
including virtually every kind of business, political and
municipal activity. Moreover, when we examine how these

entities were structured, governed and regulated we find that they bear many similarities to corporations and, indeed, to modern US corporations. The familiar concerns of agency costs and incentive effects are both present and addressed in quite similar ways as are many other aspects of the law regulating business entities. Further, examining the historical development of the śreṇi indicates that the factors leading to the growth of this corporate form are consistent with those put forward for the growth of organizational entities in Europe. These factors include increasing trade, methods to contain agency costs, and methods to patrol the boundaries between the assets of the śreṇi and those of its members (i.e., to facilitate asset partitioning and reduce creditor information costs). Finally, examination of the development of the śreṇi in Ancient India sheds light on the importance of state structure for the growth of trade and the corporate form as well as on prospects for some kind of convergence in corporate governance."

Market fundamentalism needs the corrective of a global ethic

Capitalism is now robed in the new, global organizing principle of market fundamentalism. The pathological condition is best described in the words of Aristotle in his *Politics*: "While it seems that there must be a limit to every form of wealth, in practice we find that the opposite occurs: all those engaged in acquiring goods go on increasing their coin without limit…The reason why some people get this notion into their heads may be that they are eager for life but not for the good life; so desire for life being unlimited, they desire also an unlimited amount of what [they think] enables it to go on…these people turn all skills into skills of acquiring goods, as though that were the end and everything had to serve that end."[77]

"The US still makes up nearly a third of world market cap, however, and it is more than four times as big as the second biggest country -- Japan. China has the third highest market cap in the world, followed by the UK, Hong Kong, Canada, France, and India. While India and China are still considered emerging markets by most, they both have bigger market caps than Germany!"[78]

	Country Market Cap Levels			
Country	Market Cap ($, Mil)	% of Total 12/31/09	% of Total 12/31/10	Change
World	52466373	100.00	100.00	0.00
United States	15559765	29.92	29.68	-0.23
Japan	4013490	7.59	7.69	0.10
China	3813920	7.15	7.23	0.08
United Kingdom	3389874	6.47	6.42	-0.06
Hong Kong	2579378	4.93	4.78	-0.15
Canada	2104890	3.50	4.04	0.54
France	1796545	4.13	3.38	-0.75
India	1628673	2.82	3.13	0.32
Germany	1515063	2.98	2.89	-0.09
Australia	1463179	2.73	2.85	0.13
Brazil	1457790	2.89	2.78	-0.11
Switzerland	1193428	2.34	2.31	-0.03
South Korea	1098158	1.79	2.07	0.28
Taiwan	921883	1.57	1.77	0.20
Russia	691005	1.02	1.33	0.31
Spain	630181	1.71	1.22	-0.50
Italy	604901	1.49	1.15	-0.34
Sweden	604253	0.98	1.15	0.16
Singapore	586722	0.97	1.11	0.14
South Africa	532890	0.87	1.03	0.16
Mexico	500097	0.79	0.96	0.17
Malaysia	413515	0.62	0.78	0.16
Indonesia	361820	0.46	0.69	0.22
Saudi Arabia	358730	0.69	0.68	-0.01
Chile	331719	0.50	0.65	0.16
Netherlands	327604	0.71	0.63	-0.08
Turkey	310996	0.49	0.58	0.09
Norway	289029	0.56	0.56	0.00
Thailand	277345	0.38	0.53	0.15
Belgium	272845	0.54	0.52	-0.03

"By simply dividing each country's stock market capitalization by its GDP, I was able to generate the bubble graph below. The size of the bubble indicates the size of the market cap but the key here is the Market Cap to GDP ratio as measured by the y axis…There are several reasons determining the size of a country's stock market capitalization including, for example, the equity-buying culture of the local population, company use of debt versus equity financing, the country's regulatory and legal environment as well as how easy it is to list on the local exchange. In general however, it is probably safe to assume that there should be a positive correlation between a country's market capitalization and its GDP. Indeed it turns out there is a very high, 0.96 correlation between the world's largest economies GDPs and their stock market capitalizations."[79]

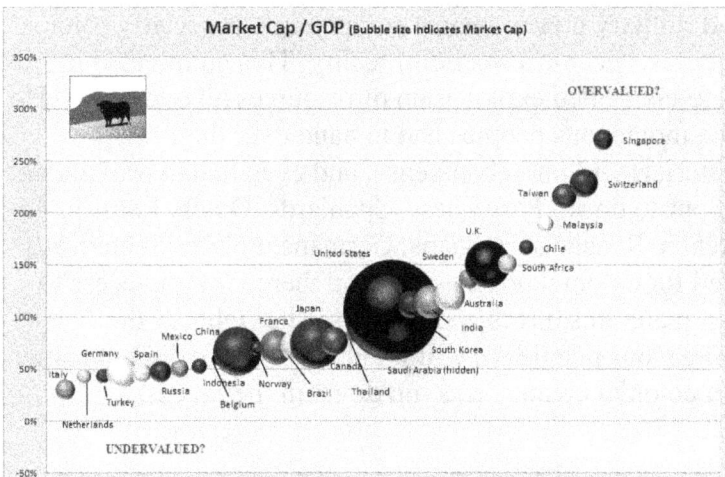

Market Cap / GDP (Bubble size indicates Market Cap)

Political economies such as India are not identifiable with capitalist or socialist/communist ideologies are tottering on the brink, rendered mute, haunted by the global specter of market fundamentalism.

John Kenneth Galbraith[80] wrote a perceptive essay in 1958 on India's impact on economic ideas. This essay has equal relevance for many other developing economies, in particular those which were subject to colonial domination and colonial loot of their wealth and are now free nations, free to evolve a self-reliant political economy regulated to tend towards full employment.

[quote] Robbery and looting – the example of Bangladesh

With the progress of industrialisation, capital accumulation intensified and with it the possibility of wielding economic and military power against competitors, especially colonial peoples, became a shameful reality. This culminated in state-controlled exploitation of resources all over the world. The indigenous peoples had to hand over their raw materials without recompense, and even had to provide the labour to do so. Portuguese, Spaniards, Dutch, English, French, Russians, Belgians, Germans, Italians, Americans vied for colonial possessions, and therewith for access to raw material sources and markets. The rights of the indigenous people were of no interest, and it did not matter if a colonial country was run down in the process.

Thus the wealth of the industrial countries was built upon the exploitation of colonial people who had to supply raw materials cheaply and then buy manufactured products made from these raw materials at high prices. Whole flourishing national economies were sacrificed to this one-sided trade, as the example of the plunder of Bengal shows.

Bengal, once called 'Golden Bengal' or the 'Paradise of the Nations', was one of the richest provinces of India, while today, as Bangladesh, it is one of the poorest nations on earth. The American academic Noam Chomsky writes in his book Year 501 (South End Press 1993) that in 1757 (the year in which Great Britain, through the British East India Company, was able to secure its ascendancy over India at the Battle of Plassey), the textile centre of Dacca was comparable to the city of London in spread, population and wealth. But by 1840, 'its population had fallen from 150,000 to 30,000, 'as Sir Charles Trevelyan testified before the Select Committee of the House of Lords, "and the jungle and malaria are fast encroaching. [...] Dacca, the Manchester of India, has fallen from a very flourishing town to a very poor and small town." [...] Bengal was known for its fine cotton, now extinct, and for the excellence of its textiles, now imported. After the British takeover, British traders, using "every conceivable form of roguery," "acquired the weavers' cloth for a fraction of its value," English merchant William Bolts wrote in 1772: "Various and innumerable are the methods of oppressing the poor weavers. [...] such as by fines, imprisonments, floggings, forcing bonds from them, etc." "The oppression and monopolies" imposed by the English "have been the causes of the decline of trade, the decrease of the revenues, and the present ruinous condition of affairs in Bengal."'

The fact that even far worse happened in other colonies, for example in the Belgian Congo, should be mentioned here only in passing. [unquote][81]

Referring to the colonial regime in India, Mahatma Gandhi said at Chatham House, London on October 20, 1931 that: "I say without fear of my figures being challenged successfully, that today India is more illiterate than it was fifty or a hundred years ago, and so is Burma, because the Brit¬ish administrators, when they came to India, instead of taking hold of things as they were, began to root them out. They scratched the soil and began to look at the root, and left the root like that, and the beautiful tree perished." The tree of the Indian education system was desiccated.[82]

One method to annihilate the beautiful tree was what Karl Marx saw, in 1853: "England has to fulfill a double mission in India: one destructive, the other regenerating—the annihilation of the old Asiatic society, and the laying of the material foundation of Western society in Asia."[83]

Another method was imposition of heavy land revenue through a total centralization and the oppressive manner in which it was collected, made most Indian farmers landless and poor. With the falling grain production, the famines became a common occurrence. Whereas in the first half of the 19th century there were seven famines with an estimated deaths of 1.5 million people, there were 24 famines with an estimated deaths of over 20 million people in the 2nd half.[84]

"At the time of arrival of the East India Company around 1700 AD, India was one of wealthiest and culturally most advanced countries in the world. India's share of the world's GDP in 1700 AD was 24.44% as compared to UK's 2.83%, China's 22.30% and USA's 0.14%. By 1913, India's share of world GDP came down to 7.55% and that of UK went up to 8.31%. At the end of the British rule in 1947, India's share of GDP fell down to 4.16% ((GDP figures based on Angus Maddison's book-'The World Economy' -2001). William Digby in his book, 'Prosperous' British India, London, 1901 mentions the drain of capital from India during the 19th century amounted to Pound Sterling 6,080,172,021 which would today work out to more than a trillion US Dollars."[85]

India may have to offer a self-reliant economic theory which will ensure full employment for large populations living in villages.

It should be recognized that, in economic history, India was the major contributor to world GDP until 1700 CE.

Galbraith began his essay on 'Rival economic theories in India' noting the immunity of Indian economy from any influence from any source: "If we are to understand the impact on India of foreign economic ideas we must first recognize how immune the Indian economy is to influence from any source, including that of the Indian Government. Indian life, as we have so often been told, resides in the villages. The great cities – Calcutta, Bombay, Delhi, Madras – are, in any quantitative sence, on the fringe of Indian society. Eight-three percnt of the people live in the villages; and these number a nearly unimaginable 612,000,000. The isolation of the Indian village is something that can be both seen and felt. The thin, searching people, the mud and thatch, the patrol of silent cows, the meager surrounding fields, all convey a sense of solitude. Village government is primitive and but slightly tied to central authority. There is no priest who is in communication with his hierarchy and no telephone or telegraph lines to the city. Often the village can be approached only on foot. Those who have approached it over the mud dikes or along the dusty paths in centuries past have been the agents of old oppressions or the harbingers of new misfortunes. At best they have been

234

bearers of promises that were never kept or prophets of reforms that were never made. Out of the depths of this experience the village has a deeply ingrained mistrust of the world outside, and this mistrust is directed first of all at those who presume to govern. The economic life of the village is concerned, indeed preoccupied, with the production of food. And so, therefore, is Indian economic life as a whole. Approximately half of India's gross national product is made in agriculture, and approximately 70 percent of the people are directly dependent on agriculture for their livelihoos. In an economy where food is so important, so, inevitably, is land. There are very few generalizations which can be made about landholding in the Indian villages. Some people own a great deal more land than others, but a great many people do own some. The state governments are trying with varying degrees of efficiency, determination and success to broaden the base of land ownership. Perhaps it is enough to say that the Indian agrarian community is one of marked but not limitless economic and social inequality. At its bottom, however, are to be found perhaps the world's most unfortunate men – the mass of landless laborers for whom idleness, hunger and privation are endemic. All in all, the

Indian village is no Auburn. The villages do not, of course, comprise the total of Indian economic life. India has long had an excellent transportation network – by far the best in Asia. There is a highly developed urban trading community. And long before Independence, India had a large and efficient cotton textile industry, the world's principal jute manufacturing industry, a small steel industry and some development in other fields. But apart from the textile mills, industry was a thin fringe. Much has been made of Indian (or Parsi) enterprise in building steel industry. But prior to Independence this had brought India only about a million tons of capacity. Canada, with colonial antecedents and only a minute fraction of India's population, had several times as much. Much of our recent attitudes toward the Indian economy have been shaped by the government activities since Independence. These have centered on the two Five Year Plans, the first of which was devoted primarily, although not exclusively, to expanding food production and particularly to the development of large and small irrigation enterprises…Even the most intransigent Indian capitalist may observe on occasion that he is really a socialist at heart. This reiterated reference to socialism is extremely important for understanding of the

236

Indian economy – or, to speak more precisely, it contributes greatly to the failure to understand it. The word socialism implies social control of the economy by the government. Five year plans carry the same connotation....Yet, by almost any test, the economy of India is less responsive to public guidance and direction than that of the United States. Indeed, it is one of the world's least controlled or 'planned' economies. In the United States the several levels of government dispose of about 20 percent of total production (of $434 billions in 1957). In India the corresponding figure is not over ten percent. By this test –the size of state activity in relation to all activity—more than twice as much of the American economy is managed or planned by government as is the case in India...Wages, hours and conditions of labor are much more extensively regulated in the United States, and in one way or another we can do more about manpower supply. Taxation and fiscal policy are subject to the same manipulation in free enterprise Washington as in socialist India, and in our case the tools in the hands of the government are almost certainly more efficient. Our industrial price-making is subject quite generally to the administration of large corporations. As a result, it is decidedly more restrained than the truly free markets of India. In the aggregate, there can be little doubt that ours is both much the more manageable and the more managed economy. India has, in fact, superimposed a smallish socialized sector atop what, no doubt, is the world's greatest example of functioning anarchy…It has long been remarked that, where economic wisdom is concerned, we have both a domestic and an export product. The domestic product is an intricate blend of pragmatism and compromise. It abhors government intervention in principle but not in practice. Social security and social insurance, a large range of subsidies and controls, a policy for containing depressions and inflation, a farm policy, and a resource development policy are all recognized to be either essential or desirable. We are categorically opposed to government intervention only when it is categorically for someone else's benefit. This social pragmatism – this accommodation to circumstance – far more than rigid adherence to doctrine accounts for what measures of economic success we have enjoyed. But the common export version of American economic policy is very different. This is a pure distillate of boisterous enterprise and undiluted laissez-faire. Rugged individualism and rigorous competition are the thing. Men who wouldn't think of taking this medicine themselves unhesitatingly prescribe it for foreigners...The misunderstanding of India lies in the failure to see the unique inapplicability of the free enterprise formula – either in its pure or diluted form – to that country. As noted, the Indian commitment to the semantics of socialism is at least as deep as ours to the semantics of free enterprise...And until recent times a good deal of capitalist enterprise in India was an extension of the arm of the imperial power – indeed, in part its confessed *raison d'etre*...Did India lag behind the West in the last century and the early part of this one because the British repressed growth or because of more deeply seated causes? If more deeply seated and enduring factors prevented rapid development in the great age of enterrise, then to count on free enterprise now would be a dreadful risk...There are also the social consequences of capitalism to reckon with. Left to itself, as the specifications would require, capitalism is a system of manifest inequality. Inequality has ceased to be a thing of great social urgency in a country where opulence is general. It still has grave and even revolutionary implications in a country where nearly everyone is poor and where many are hungry. Anyone who is familiar with India will also be aware of the talent of its people for conspicuous consumption.[86] This is a part of the world where the rich are rarely discreet...Unemployment compensation, old age insurance, farm price guarantees, and the numerous other ways by which we blunt the sharp edges of the capitalist machinery for th ordinary citizen, also helps to make tolerable the wealth of the well-to-do. These social luxuries are also unavailable to the Indian Government...At the same time it is becoming increasingly clear that Indian economic policy is at its best when it is most self-reliant. Adaptation of action to circumstances has on numerous occasions produced better results than the adoption of foreign models...Perhaps the greatest unsolved problem of the Indians is to find some way to insure efficient public entrepreneurship under the general aegis of a parliamentary government..."

European Community and Indian Ocean Community as Rāṣṭram[87], grouping of nations

Such political economies like India's which have stood the test of time for over two millennia, have the potential to offer a global ethic for decentralized institutions consistent with a relativist theory of wealth of nations. The grouping of nations is *raṣṭrī* a lighted path for welfare of people and acquisition of wealth, *vasu*.

aham raṣṭrī samgamanī vasūnām (RV 10.125). I am the rastram carrying along wealth of people

- *dhruvám te rājā váruṇo*
  dhruvám devó bŕhaspátiḥ
  dhruvám ta índraś cāgníś ca
  rāṣṭrám dhārayatām dhruvám (RV 10.173.5)

- Steadfast, may Varuṇa, the Rājā, steadfast, the Divine Bṛhaspati steadfast, may Indra, steadfast too, may Agni keep they steadfast Rāṣṭram. In this Rgvedic statement, Rāṣṭram is emphasized as the epitome of 'steadfastness'. *Vājasneyi Samhitā* has a remarkable refrain which is the epitome of the characteristic of the state's role in economics:

241

Āpah parivahiṇī stha Rāṣṭradā Rāṣṭram me datta svāhā
Āpah parivahiṇī stha Rāṣṭradā Rāṣṭramamuṣmai datta
svāhā

> *Rāṣṭram* is a firm well-endowed path with skilled
> workers, bountiful waters, beneficial environment,
> for welfare for generations, *amuṣmika.*

Coupled with economic theory founded on the household,
these founding principles for *Rāṣṭram* (European
Community or Indian Ocean Commmunity as examples),
the effulgent path for carrying along the people on the path
of welfare is a sacred ordinance.

State intervention can act as an antidote to the evils of
market fundamentalism. The economic multiplier effect
creating the wealth of nations will be phenomenal in such
grouping of nations.

This intervention can take two forms:

1. Formations of federating nations as free markets
   such as European Community or Indian Ocean
   Community

2. Decentralisation of economi decision-making to
   local communities to maximize employment
   opportunities and to promote self-reliance.

242

European Union Member States

Indian Ocean Community

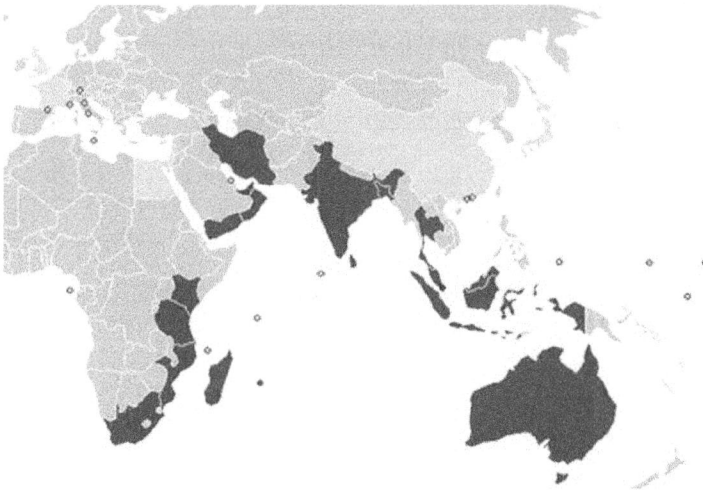

About the author

Dr. S. Kalyanaraman is Director, Sarasvati Research Center, President, Ramasetu Protection Movement in India and BoD member of World Association for Vedic Studies. His research interests relate to rediscovery of Vedic Sarasvati River, roots of Hindu civilization, decoding of Indus Script, National Water Grid and creation of Indian Ocean Community. He has a Ph.D. in Public Administration from the University of the Philippines. He is a multi-lingual scholar versed in Tamil, Telugu, Kannada, Sanskrit, Hindi. He was a senior financial and IT executive in Asian Development Bank, Manila, Philippines and on Indian Railways. His 18 publications include: Indian Lexicon - a multilingual dictionary for over 25 Indian languages, Sarasvati in 15 volumes, Indian Alchemy - Soma in the Veda, Indus Script Cipher, Rastram, Indian Hieroglyphs, Indian Ocean Community. He is a recipient of many awards including Vakankar Award (2000), Shivananda Eminent Citizens' Award (2008) and Dr. Hedgewar Prajna Samman (2008).

Website: http://sites.google.com/site/kalyan97

About the book

A theory for wealth of nations -- Market economics
overturns Adam Smith and Karl Marx

In the context of economic theories of political economy,
market capitalism dominated by a network of corporations
defines global capitalism which makes society subservient.
Economic history of two millennia provide a framework for
delineating a relativist theory for wealth of nations
governed by Śreṇi dharma to cope with greed and
corruption. The metaphor of varaha, upholding the earth
provides an outline for sustaining wealth of nations.
Reviewing humanist-ethical development models and role
of social capital, the dominant role has to be assigned to
household economics which provides for rebuilding
economic theory founded on a global ethic to correct
market fundamentalism and to create and strengthen
European Community and Indian Ocean Community as
Rāṣṭram, grouping of nations. Such a theory will promote
and sustain wealth of the grouped nations.

Index

accountability, 15, 17

Africa, 63, 65, 67, 68, 70, 72, 74, 77, 86, 87, 88, 90, 91, 93, 94, 95

agriculture, 47, 65, 71, 73, 80, 81, 129, 130, 209, 235

America, 11, 63, 65, 66, 74, 76, 77, 88, 91, 104

artha, 101, 109, 157, 194, 197, 220, 221

Asia, 45, 59, 65, 67, 68, 70, 72, 74, 77, 85, 86, 87, 88, 93, 94, 95, 98, 106, 232, 236

body, 111

bonds, 4, 12, 20, 77, 84, 231

borrowing, 19, 85

capital market, 76

central bank, 223

China, 94

communism, 4, 10, 101

compensation, 17, 240

competition, 17, 49, 73, 212, 239

consumption, 39, 71, 104, 240

corporation, 58, 147, 148, 149, 151, 152, 153, 199, 225

corruption, 3, 147, 148, 151, 154, 157, 245

culture, 213, 229

debt, 4, 12, 14, 19, 35, 39, 45, 48, 76, 85, 229

default, 11, 19, 20, 83, 143

democracy, 155

depression, 15, 79, 83, 84

derivative, 6, 7, 12, 13, 20, 21, 27, 38

developing, 6, 36, 37, 38, 49, 68, 69, 81, 87, 89, 230

dharma, 111

earth, 3, 78, 101, 105, 113, 114, 115, 124, 126, 131, 159, 161, 164, 165, 168, 169, 170, 171, 180, 183, 186, 192, 231, 245

economic theory, 3, 10, 37, 43, 50, 99, 159, 220, 233, 242, 245

education, 56, 60, 72, 75, 209, 232

employment, 48, 157, 218, 230, 233, 242

environment, 161, 229

equity, 229

euro, 48, 248

Europe, 47, 62, 65, 67, 68, 70, 71, 72, 77, 79, 80, 83, 84, 86, 87, 89, 94, 140, 226

free market, 35, 36, 238, 242

global economy, 54

global financial system, 13

globalization, 43, 59, 211

gold, 43, 76, 118, 137, 139, 164, 168, 170, 176, 183, 186, 190

happiness, 57, 103, 135, 199, 211

health, 12, 200, 206, 209

Hindu, 111

IMF, 35, 50, 58

India, 74, 75, 78, 85, 94, 112, 121, 125, 130, 143, 147, 200, 204, 207, 208, 209, 211, 219, 223, 224, 225, 227, 230, 231, 232, 233, 234, 241, 244

Indian Ocean, 3, 47, 49, 68, 91, 93, 95, 98, 148, 151, 152, 157,

205, 206, 241, 242, 243, 244, 245

inequality, 225, 235

inflation, 55, 83, 156, 238

innovation, 56, 64, 81, 209, 213, 214

instability, 26, 42

interdependence, 106

justice, 44, 50, 54, 113, 128, 132, 148, 152, 194, 209

legal, 124, 152, 229

pace, 93, 98

profit, 12, 19, 38, 39, 76, 138, 212, 223

property right, 72, 76, 225

Sarasvati, 1, 2

sovereign, 10, 19

technology, 45, 56, 64, 67, 70, 76, 78, 86, 150, 223

textiles, 90, 138, 231

Vedic, 110

World bank, 32

End Notes

---

[1] BIS Quarterly Review, December 2008
http://www.bis.org/publ/qtrpdf/r_qa0812.pdf

[2] www.Bis.org

[3] Nicholas Chan, Mila Getmansky, Shane M. Haas, Andrew W. Lo, 2005, Systemic risk and hedge funds, NBER Working Paper No. 11200 issued in March 2005
http://www.nber.org/papers/w11200

[4] Raghuram G. Rajan (September 2006). "Has Financial Development Made the World Riskier?". European Financial Management 12 (4): 499-533.

[5] http://en.wikipedia.org/wiki/Stock_market

[6] http://www.occ.gov/topics/capital-markets/financial-markets/trading/derivatives/dq311.pdf

[7] http://www.reuters.com/article/2012/02/09/eu-derivatives-idUSL5E8D969P20120209 [quote] In the past, it has been common for multi-million-euro contracts to be recorded by no more than a fax, with only the parties involved aware of the details. This will change under the new law, which would standardise most trading so it happens on open exchanges. Settlement of such deals will be cleared centrally, making them easier to monitor. Those that do not shift to exchanges or a central counterparty such as LCH Clearnet in London, which acts as an intermediary between buyer and seller, will face higher capital charges to reflect

the extra risk. Crucially, the new rules mean that all deals must be recorded, whether conducted on or off an exchange. Supervisors hope that will make it easier to monitor the market and intervene, if necessary, to avoid a repeat of the chaos surrounding the 2008 collapse of Lehman Brothers, where it proved difficult to assess exposure to derivatives...Some analysts see risks in the new regime and think regulators will be overwhelmed by trying to follow such a huge market. "By centrally clearing trades, you concentrate risk dramatically into one body, such as a central counterparty," said Graham Bishop, who advises banks on European financial policy. "We have to be careful these bodies don't become a financial nuclear bomb." [unquote]

8

http://www.wanttoknow.info/banking_finance/derivatives_market_bubble_financial

[9] http://www.rediff.com/money/2005/apr/19perfin1.htm

[10] 1849, Occasional Discourse on the Negro question. "Not a "gay science," I should say, like some we have heard of; no, a dreary, desolate and, indeed, quite abject and distressing one; what we might call, by way of eminence, the *dismal science*." It was "dismal" in "find[ing] the secret of this Universe in 'supply and demand,' and reducing the duty of human governors to that of letting men alone." Instead, the "idle Black man in the West Indies" should be "*compelled* to work as he was fit, and to*do* the Maker's will who had constructed him." [As quoted in Joseph Persky,

1990. "Retrospectives: A Dismal Romantic," *Journal of Economic Perspectives*, 4(4), pp. 167-169 [pp. 165-172].

[11] Keen, S., 2001, Debunking Economics, Pluto Press. M. Christopher Auld, 2002, Debunking 'Debunking Economics', http://www.econ.canterbury.ac.nz/personal_pages/paul_walker/debunk.pdf

[12] Author of *An Inquiry into the Nature and Causes of the Wealth of Nations* (1776).

[13] Author of *The Communist Manifesto* (1848).

[14] The term was used by Colin Leys and Edward Lewis in a two part essay based on Edward Lewis' interview of Colin Leys, an honorary professor of economics a Goldsmiths College London (May 2010). http://www.newleftproject.org/index.php/site/article_comments/the_dictatorship_of_the_market_-_part_2 Daniel J. Mitchell had used the term, 'pseudo-dictatorship of the Market' in 2007 critical of French President Nicolas Sarkozy's failure to liberalize France's economy and reduce the burden of government. http://www.cato-at-liberty.org/the-pseudo-dictatorship-of-the-market/

[15] http://en.wikipedia.org/wiki/The_Cluetrain_Manifesto

16

http://topics.nytimes.com/top/reference/timestopics/subjects/d/derivatives/index.html

[17] http://www.businessweek.com/articles/2012-09-11/a-4-trillion-dodd-frank-loophole

18

http://www.americanprogress.org/issues/regulation/report/2012/07/20/11910/dodd-frank-financial-reform-after-2-years/

19

http://en.wikipedia.org/wiki/Derivative_(finance)#cite_note-22

20

http://en.wikipedia.org/wiki/Dodd%E2%80%93Frank_Wall_Street_Reform_and_Consumer_Protection_Act

[21] Senate Committee on Banking, Housing, and Urban Affairs, Chairman Chris Dodd (D-CT) http://banking.senate.gov/public/_files/FinancialReformSummaryAsFiled.pdf

[22] Michael Simikovic, 2011, Competition and crisis in mortgage securitization, *Indiana Law Journal*, Vol. 88, 2013. http://papers.ssrn.com/sol3/papers.cfm?abstract_id=1924831

[23] Confer Thomas Philippon: "The future of the financial industry", Finance Department of the New York University Stern School of Business at New York University http://pages.stern.nyu.edu/~sternfin/crisis/

[24] http://www.usnews.com/opinion/blogs/economic-intelligence/2012/07/16/derivatives-should-be-banned-from-financial-markets

25

http://demonocracy.info/infographics/usa/derivatives/bank_exposure.html

26

http://en.wikipedia.org/wiki/Moneyness#ITM:_In_the_money http://en.wikipedia.org/wiki/Derivative_(finance)

[27] http://visualizingeconomics.com/blog/2009/01/11/stock-market-world-gdp-statistical-data-sculptures

28

http://www.economist.com/blogs/freeexchange/2012/09/derivatives-markets-regulation

[29] http://www.economist.com/node/21560563 See Morris, Stephen; Shin, Hyun Song (1999). "Risk management with interdependent choice". *Oxford Review of Economic Policy* **15** (3): 52–62. " In normal times the market behaves like a game of roulette; the probabilities are known and largely independent of the investment decisions of the different players. In times of market stress, however, the game becomes more like poker (herding behavior takes over). The players now must give heavy weight to the psychology of other investors and how they are likely to react psychologically."
http://en.wikipedia.org/wiki/Stock_market#cite_ref-17

252

[30] Gevit Duca (Univ. of Malta), The relationship between stock market and the economy: experience from international financial markets, Bank of Valetta Review, No. 36, Autumn 2007
http://www.bov.com/filebank/documents/1-12_Gevit%20Duca.pdf

[31] Designation as an "Emerging Market" by Dow Jones 2010

Value multiples derived from various country ETFs as listed by Morningstar.

[32] http://seekingalpha.com/article/250102-which-country-s-stock-market-is-the-most-expensive

[33] http://www.tradingeconomics.com/world/market-capitalization-of-listed-companies-percent-of-gdp-wb-data.html

34

http://www.virtus.com/vsitemanager/upload/docs/6141_gdpwhitepaper.pdf

35

http://us.bnymellonam.com/core/library/documents/knowledge/AlphaTrends/Stock_Markets_vs_GDP.pdf

[36] http://www.bbc.co.uk/news/magazine-17344386

[37] An open letter, July 2, 2002 to Joseph Stiglitz.
http://www.imf.org/external/np/vc/2002/070202.htm

38

http://www.investopedia.com/terms/i/imperfectmarket.asp#axzz2ENT4EVwe

[39] The global crisis and the decline of market fundamentalism Prof. Dr. Rumen Georgiev - 8/18/2011 http://www.globalpolitician.com/27038-global-recession-crisis-depression

[40] Eisuke Sakakibara, 1999, The End of Market Fundamentalism http://cas.umkc.edu/econ/Institutional/Readings/Eisuke/fundamentalism.html

[41] A nickname given to the economies of Southeast Asia.

42

http://en.wikipedia.org/wiki/1998_Russian_financial_crisis

[43] David Leinweber, 2009, *Nerds on Wall Street*, New Jersey, John Wiley & Sons, http://nerdsonwallstreet.com/stock-market-manipulations-384/

[44] Created as an European Economic Community by Treaty of Rome of 1957.

45

http://www.fese.be/_lib/files/EUROPEAN_EXCHANGE_REPORT_2011_FINAL.pdf European Exchange Report of FESE.

46

http://fese.eu/_mdb/posdocs/FESE%20SME_final.docx.pdf

[47] http://ec.europa.eu/enterprise/policies/sme/facts-figures-analysis/performance-review/files/supporting-documents/2012/annual-report_en.pdf

48

http://en.wikipedia.org/wiki/Economy_of_the_European_Union

[49] Dani Rodrik in *The New Republic*, November 2, 1998

[50] J. Habermas, Modernity an Incomplete Project, in Hal Foster, ed., *The Anti-Aesthetic: Essays on Postmodern Culture* (Port Townsend, WA: Bay Press, 1983), 3-15. http://www.aphotostudent.com/wp-content/uploads/2009/11/habermas_modernityproject.pdfJ.

51

http://arxiv.org/PS_cache/arxiv/pdf/1107/1107.5728v2.pdf

[52] OECD (2000) The OECD Guidelins for Multinational Enterprises (www.oecd.org).

[53] http://www.treehugger.com/corporate-responsibility/proof-of-global-domination-by-a-few-corporations.html

[54] E. P. Thompson, 1993, *Customs in Common: Studies in Traditional Popular Culture*, p. 188 http://understandingsociety.blogspot.co.uk/2008/07/moral-economy-as-historical-social.html

[55]Stiglitz, Joseph. *Redefining the Role of the State - What should it do ? How should it do it ? And how should these decisions be made?* Paper presented at the Tenth Anniversary of MITI Research Institute, Tokyo, March 1998. Pp.21-22 "The theories that I (and others) helped develop explained why unfettered markets often not only do not lead to social justice, but do not even produce efficient outcomes. Interestingly, there has been no intellectual challenge to the refutation of Adam Smith's invisible hand: individuals and firms, in the pursuit of their self-interest, are not necessarily, or in general, led as if by an invisible hand, to economic efficiency."
STIGLITZ, Joseph E. *The pact with the devil.* Beppe Grillo's Friends interview http://www.beppegrillo.it/eng/2007/01/stiglitz.html In this sense, *the fall of Wall Street is for market fundamentalism what the fall of the Berlin Wall was for communism*—it tells the world that this way of economic organization turns out not to be sustainable. In the end, everyone says, that model doesn't work. Actually the model only failed the citizens, while working perfectly in ensuring profits for the Wall Street financial groups that run the USA, so privatising gain and socialising the risk when the markets fail to work as hoped. This moment is a marker that the claims of financial market liberalization were bogus.— Joseph E. Stiglitz: "The Fall of Wall Street Is to Market Fundamentalism What the Fall of the Berlin Wall Was to Communism", Interview with Nathan Gardels, The Huffington Post, September 16th 2008

[56] http://www.greattransformations.org/21st-century-economics

[57] Kozul-Wright, Richard and Rayment, Paul. *The Resistible Rise of Market Fundamentalism: Rethinking Development Policy in an Unbalanced World*. London: Zed Books Ltd, 2007 p. 14 and Chapter 6

58

http://cas.umkc.edu/econ/Institutional/Readings/Eisuke/fundamentalism.html

[59] Angus Maddison, 2001, *The world economy, a millennial perspective*, OECD, p.17
http://theunbrokenwindow.com/Development/MADDISON%20The%20World%20Economy--A%20Millennial.pdf

60

http://www.economist.com/blogs/graphicdetail/2012/06/mis-charting-economic-history

[61]http://www.ggdc.net/Maddison/other_books/Contours_World_Economy.pdf

62

http://aric.adb.org/pdf/aeim/AEIM_2012July_FullReport.pdf Asian Economic Integration Monitor, July 2012, Asian Development Bank, Manila.

[63] *Baudhāyana-dharmasūtra*, various eds 1884, 1934 (=Ba). Transl by G.Bühler, SBE XIV, reprint 1965.

Nāradasmṛti (= N, from now on), Biblioteca Indica, 1885.

Transl J. Jolly, *The Minor Lawbooks*, SBE (= Sacred Books

of the East), XXXIII, ed 1965, pp 207 ff. Also, *Nārada-dharma-śāstra*.4 XIX, 24-26, *Bṛhaspati-smṛti* (=Bṛ) ed by A.Furher, Leipsig 1879, Transl J. Jolly, as note 3, SBE XXXIII, p 254. Also, *Bṛhaspati-dharma-śāstra*. Numerous editions of Manu's lawbook, known also as *Mānavadharma-śāstra* (=M). Transl by G.Bühler, SBE XXV, reprint 1982.

Bhattacharya, A.K., 1989, Modern Accounting Concepts in Kautilya's Arthashastra, Calcutta, KLM Private Ltd.

P.Banerjee, *Public Administration* ..., London 1916, p179

Romesh Dutt, *The Economic History of India*, Delhi 1960, Vol I

KP Jayaswal, *Hindu Polity*, (Patna 1924) Bangalore 1967, passim

*Kautilya's Arthaśāstra (*Statecraft) R P Kangle's edition, Pt I, Univ Bombay, 1965. The latin numeral is chapter, the next is section and the last the sūtra (s). Kangle has published a PtII, translation, and a PtIII, a study of the work. It is commonly ascribed to Kautilya, Chief Minister of Emperor Candragupta at the end of C4th BC. Edition &

transl by R.P. Kangle in 3 vols, Bombay, 1965.
http://papers.ssrn.com/sol3/papers.cfm?abstract_id=142572
0 Appraising Accounting and Business Concepts in
Kautilya's Arthaśāstra Manjula Shyam and Shyam Sunder
Yale University - School of Management *12th World
Congress of Accounting Historians, Istanbul, Turkey, July
20-24, 2008*

Nicholas Kazanas, 2010, *Economic Principles of the Vedic
Tradition*, Aditya Prakashan, Delhi

S.K Maity, *The Economic Life of Nothern India* ..., Calcutta
1957, p25 R.C Majumdar, *The Corporate Life in Ancient
India,* Calcutta 1933, pp183-193

Mattessich, Richard, 1998, 'Review and extension of
Bhattacharya's Modern Accounting Concepts in Kautilya's
Arthashastra'. Accounting, Businessd and Financial
History, Vol. 8, No. 2. Reprinted in Mattessich, The
Beginning of Accounting and Accounting Thought, New
York, Garland Publishing, 2000.

S Nigam, *Economic Organisation in Ancient India*, M
Manoharlal, Delhi, 1975.

V.Smith, *Oxford History Of India*, OUP 1922, p90

Winternitz, vol II (HIL), transl by Subhadra Jha, Delhi, 1985, pp 575-607. Also, P. V. Kane, *History of the Dharmaśastra*, vols I-V, Poona, 1930-1962, passim.

[64] Yosef Yitzhak Lifshitz, 2004, Foundations of Jewish Economic Theory, *Azure*, Autumn 5765, p.57 http://www.azure.org.il/download/magazine/154AZ18_Y.Y._Lifshitz.pdf

[65] Henry David Thoreau

[66] Mahabharata Santi Parva, Section CCXLI Tr. Kisari Mohan Ganguli

[67] Adi S'ankara (Gita Bhashyam)

[68] *Hymns of the Atharva Veda*, by Ralph T.H. Griffith, [1895], http://www.sacred-texts.com/hin/av/av12001.htm

[69] Rene Guenon (aka Sheikh 'Abd Al Wahid Yahya), *Introduction to the Study of Hindu Doctrines*.

[70] Volume I, p.543.

[71] Source: Statement 11.1, pp 16. National Accounts Statistics (NAS) – 2011, Central Statistical Organization (CSO), Govt. of India, New Delhi

[72] Arthur Gobineau, *The inequality of human race*, 1915, First French edition, Paris, 1853-1855, 4 vol. http://archive.org/details/inequalityofhuma00gobi

[73] The very concept of capital is derived from this way of looking at things; one can say that capital, as a category, did not exist before double-entry bookkeeping. Capital can be defined as that amount of wealth which is used in making profits and which enters into the accounts." Lane, Frederic C; Riemersma, Jelle, eds. (1953). *Enterprise and Secular Change: Readings in Economic History.* R. D. Irwin. p. 38.(quoted in "Accounting and rationality")

[74] 'Fascism should more appropriately be called Corporatism because it is a merger of state and corporate power.' – Benito Mussolini (1883-1945).

[75] Stiglitz, Joseph. Redefining the Role of the State - What should it do ? How should it do it ? And how should these decisions be made? Paper presented at the Tenth Anniversary of MITI Research Institute, Tokyo, March 1998. "The theories that I (and others) helped develop explained why unfettered markets often not only do not lead to social justice, but do not even produce efficient outcomes. Interestingly, there has been no intellectual challenge to the refutation of Adam Smith's invisible hand: individuals and firms, in the pursuit of their self-interest, are not necessarily, or in general, led as if by an invisible hand, to economic efficiency." STIGLITZ, Joseph E. *The pact with the devil.* Beppe Grillo's Friends interview http://www.beppegrillo.it/eng/2007/01/stiglitz.html In this

sense, *the fall of Wall Street is for market fundamentalism what the fall of the Berlin Wall was for communism*—it tells the world that this way of economic organization turns out not to be sustainable. In the end, everyone says, that model doesn't work. Actually the model only failed the citizens, while working perfectly in ensuring profits for the Wall Street financial groups that run the USA, so privatising gain and socialising the risk when the markets fail to work as hoped. This moment is a marker that the claims of financial market liberalization were bogus.— Joseph E. Stiglitz: "The Fall of Wall Street Is to Market Fundamentalism What the Fall of the Berlin Wall Was to Communism", Interview with Nathan Gardels, The Huffington Post, September 16th 2008

76

http://papers.ssrn.com/sol3/papers.cfm?abstract_id=796464 Vikramaditya S. Khanna, 2005, *The Economic History of the Corporate Form in Ancient India*, University of Michigan Law School November 1, 2005

[77] Aristotle (trans. T.A. Sinclair), 1962, *The Politics*. Penguin Books, 1 viii 1256b26, l.ix. pp. 79-82; cf. (trans. J.A.K. Thomson), 1976, *The Ethics of Aristotle*, London, Penguin Books.

78

http://www.bespokeinvest.com/thinkbig/2011/1/5/country-market-caps.html

[79] http://seekingalpha.com/article/250102-which-country-s-stock-market-is-the-most-expensive See also: http://data.worldbank.org/indicator/CM.MKT.TRAD.GD.ZS

http://data.worldbank.org/indicator/BX.KLT.DINV.CD.WD

[80] John Kenneth Galbraith, 1958, Rival Economic Theories in India, Foreign Affairs, Vol. 36, No. 4 (July 1948), pp. 587-596

[81] http://www.grailworld.com/issues/27/economic-crisis-and-%E2%80%98global-conspiracy%E2%80%99-background-aberrations-evidence-today-%E2%80%93-overview

[82] Dharampal, 1983, The beautiful tree: indigenous Indian education in the Eighteenth century, Delhi, Biblia Impex

[83] First published in New York Daily Tribune, August 8, 1853.

[84] The History & Culture of the Indian People-volume ten- R.C. Majumdar, 1996

[85] Dhiru Shah summarizing Dharampal's work (2012). http://bharatkalyan97.blogspot.in/2012/12/the-beautiful-tree-historical.html

[86] With 300 million consumers (out of world population of nearly 7 billion in 2011), US imports totaled $1.6 trillion (i.e. 12.7% of the world share). China alone exported $364.9 billion worth of goods to US in 2010. Compare these numbers with the East India Company as a trading company which was nationalized in 1874 by Britain in the wake of the Great Indian War of Independence, 1857 (referred to derisively as Indian Mutiny, from an imperialist perspective.) William Henry Pyne notes in his book *The Microcosm of London* (1808) that: "On the 1 March 1801, the debts of the East India Company to £5,393,989 their effects to £15,404,736 and their sales increased since February 1793, from £4,988,300 to £7,602,041." http://en.wikipedia.org/wiki/East_India_Company

[87] Kalyanaraman, S., 2012, Indian Ocean Community, Herndon, VA, Sarasvati Research Center.

www.ingramcontent.com/pod-product-compliance
Lightning Source LLC
Chambersburg PA
CBHW061157240326

R18026500001B/R180265PG41519CBX00021B/35